Beethoven's Chamber Music

Unlocking the Masters Series, No. 24

Series Editor: Robert Levine

Beethoven's
Chamber Music
A Listener's Guide

Victor Lederer

AMADEUS
PRESS

An Imprint of Hal Leonard Corporation

Published in 2012 by Amadeus Press
An Imprint of Hal Leonard Corporation
7777 West Bluemound Road
Milwaukee, WI 53213

Trade Book Division Editorial Offices
33 Plymouth St., Montclair, NJ 07042

Printed in the United States of America

Book design by Snow Creative Services

Library of Congress Cataloging-in-Publication Data

Lederer, Victor.
  Beethoven's chamber music : a listener's guide / Victor Lederer.
    p. cm. — (Unlocking the masters series ; no. 24)
  Includes bibliographical references.
  ISBN 978-1-57467-203-9
  1. Beethoven, Ludwig van, 1770–1827. Chamber music. 2. Chamber music–19th century–History and criticism. I. Title.
  ML410.B4L2927 2012
  785.0092—dc23
                                                                    2012002953

www.amadeuspress.com

For Alan Redner

Contents

Acknowledgments

Thanks to the usual: my family, Elaine, Paul, and Karen; my editor and friend Bob Levine; and Bernie Rose for his help on technical matters.

Beethoven's
Chamber Music

Beethoven's Chamber Music

For the novice listener, no matter how eager, Beethoven's works for chamber ensembles might seem the most challenging of his output. The symphonies, appealingly grand in scale, are decked out in the splendor of the full orchestra, and pretty familiar at least in part from their common role in our culture. Everyone knows the da-da-da-*dumm* of the Fifth Symphony as well as parts of the Ninth—notably, the exciting opening phrase of the second movement (with its unforgettable timpani solo) and some of the choral finale can be heard, albeit in fragments, all around us, even in television commercials. Some of Beethoven's music for piano—the little bagatelle "Für Elise" and the arching melody of the slow movement of the "Pathétique" Sonata, not to mention the familiar sound of the instrument itself, are also helpful in easing the way into that category. But who will recognize a bar or two from one of the sonatas for piano and cello, or one of the string quartets, apart from professional musicians and a cult-like class of dedicated listeners? Without doubt, chamber music as a category has an insider quality that sets it apart.

Moreover, as the musical arenas for which composers beginning with Haydn have reserved some of their noblest ideas, there's little doubt that chamber compositions tend to be serious rather than showy. The private or semiprivate settings in which chamber music was first performed surely drew composers naturally toward the expression of their most personal ideas. And since chamber music is a conversation among just a few instruments, it's inherently unlike the public musical contest that is the concerto. Beethoven's music is, of course, some of the most widely loved and respected by any composer, and many of his works for chamber ensembles—in his case from two to seven instrumental players—is considered as being at the very peak of his achievement. So it's incumbent on the listener who wants a comprehensive understanding of Beethoven's work to acquaint himself or herself with this crucial category. Keep in mind that chamber music is essentially a kind of intimate dialogue among the instruments, and some, such as the sonatas for piano and violin and those for piano and cello, are virtuoso showpieces, not that different in character from the piano sonatas. These works for two instruments also display that wild energy for which Beethoven is famous and which makes them recognizable as his, and therefore perhaps more immediately engaging to listen to. On the other hand, much of the chamber music, chiefly the string quartets, which are the high-water mark of the composer's work for small ensembles, is undeniably intense, often cerebral. Of course no one can replicate the mix of intellect, emotion, and creative energy that allowed Beethoven to compose this astonishing music. But if you listen imaginatively—remembering that, as complex as his musical textures may get, Beethoven rarely hides his feelings—you should do well. It has been observed that chamber music is more enjoyable for the players to perform, in their quest for perfect ensemble—meaning how well they play together—than for listeners to hear, but that really only applies to dull performances. There are ways into this music, and the rewards it offers are enormous.

Perhaps the name of the category, burdened with the archaic-sounding word "chamber," puts people off, and *ensemble music* or another less fussy phrase might make potential listeners less uneasy. The name is a literal but unfortunate translation of the word *camera*, meaning "chamber," a verbal element in one of those pragmatic and descriptive Italian terms that sometimes translate badly into English. Thus, a *sonata da camera* defines an instrumental composition to be played in a domestic room (or chamber), as opposed to a *sonata da chiesa*, performed by instruments during intervals in church (*chiesa*) services. A *sonata*—from *sonare*, "to sound"—is itself a piece played, or sounded, on an instrument or group of instruments; its companion is the *cantata*—from *cantare*, "to sing," which defines while describing a musical work that's sung. In any case, the term carries little of its original sense, since most listeners who hear chamber music performed live do so in concert halls, sometimes even large ones.

Few admirers of chamber music are likely to dispute that compositions for small ensembles reached many of their highest peaks with Haydn, Mozart, and Beethoven; but the list of great and fine works in this category both before and after the Viennese big three (all worked in Vienna, the era's musical nerve center) is also long and distinguished. All kinds of genres for small combinations of instruments emerged in the seventeenth century with ensemble pieces by terrific composers such as Henry Purcell in England, Arcangelo Corelli in Italy, and François Couperin in France. Titans of the late baroque who were active in the field included Jean-Philippe Rameau, George Frideric Handel, and Johann Sebastian Bach. Rameau's music, vivid and charming but not without power, sadly belongs to baroque specialists, although it deserves the widest audience. A bit generic, Handel's chamber works make up a minor portion of that master's oeuvre. Bach's chamber music, on the other hand, comprises some of his finest efforts, including the astonishing works for solo violin and cello. Also by Bach are sonatas for harpsichord and viola da gamba, a precursor and relative of the cello with an interesting and somewhat mournful metallic timbre, and sonatas for harpsichord and violin that are also of major dimension and weight. Bach composed some trio sonatas, more decorative pieces for other ensembles that are somewhat less ambitious but of course quite beautiful on their own terms. Bach's chamber works for violin and gamba display a parity between the string and the keyboard "accompaniments" that anticipates what later composers would strive for. Even though Beethoven admired Bach deeply (and Handel, too), the earlier master's influence on him in this field is hard to detect.

The influence of Franz Josef Haydn on both Wolfgang Amadeus Mozart and Beethoven is, however, absolutely clear. This amiable giant, who was Mozart's friend and admirer and Beethoven's teacher, composed hundreds of pieces for a variety of chamber ensembles, of which the two most important are the string quartet, a genre he created in the 1750s, and the trio for piano, violin, and cello, which is called the piano trio. The quartet is quite simply the most significant genre of chamber music, into which Haydn and Beethoven poured their best efforts. (Mozart's ten mature string quartets stand on the same level, as do five of the six string quintets and several other chamber works.) Haydn composed eighty-three string quartets. The mature works, beginning with those published in 1781 as Op. 33, are all masterpieces, and there are more than forty of these, each with its singular musical message. (The violinist Hans Keller analyzed the *forty-five* Haydn quartets he considered the best in a worthwhile book.)[1] Much more about structure will follow in the chapters about Beethoven's quartets; but Haydn's four-movement format was the one adopted, at least initially, by Mozart, Beethoven, and most of the composers who followed them; Beethoven would expand it considerably. Haydn's piano trios form another important, albeit less accessible segment of the repertory. The piano dominates these wonderful pieces, so the three instruments are not equal partners, as they would be in trios by later composers. But Haydn's imagination really soars in these great compositions, which, like much of that master's work, demand that the listener retune his or her ears to a different sound and scale.

It might be an exaggeration to credit Haydn with inventing the high classical style, but only a slight one. Born in 1732, Haydn entered the European musical scene during one of its weakest phases—what we now call the early classical era, when the grandeur of the high baroque had yielded to the charming but thin *galant* and rococo of the mid-eighteenth century. Other composers of quality were Christoph Willibald Gluck, an earnest if limited musician whose opera *Orfeo ed Euridice* marked a move away from the excesses of the operas of the day and toward a more streamlined, dramatically truthful style; and J. S. Bach's sons Johann Christian and the excellent Carl Philipp Emanuel, who possessed greater technical skills than Gluck but were sometimes mired in the fundamental triviality of the era's style. Haydn's boldness and originality seem to tower above them all. But for modern listeners, his intricate, witty style is more difficult to grasp than Mozart's seductiveness or Beethoven's power, which carry us along more easily. He rarely builds to climaxes over long spans, like his successors, working instead over short or moderate periods, playing with his themes by distorting rhythms and harmonies. His music speaks to the intellect as much as to the emotions. One may not always be prepared to give

Haydn's music the attention it needs, but when in the right frame of mind, it is irresistible.

Haydn transformed the bland and trite melodic formulas of the early classical era into pithy themes rich in individual, even eccentric character. Mozart turned them into long-limbed, aristocratic tunes, typically with an operatic flavor. He also added rich harmonic underpinnings that pull toward melancholy and polished his exteriors to a tonal sheen that few others have ever achieved. Finally, he began to build individual movements of instrumental works and numbers in his operas along longer lines, and even to employ thematic elements that structured the large-scale works into a dramatic unity. Perhaps the most remarkable examples can be found in the mature operas *Don Giovanni* and *Così fan tutte*, where Mozart presents themes in the overtures that reappear later as mottoes for ideas or events; their recurrences, overwhelming in effect, anticipate the thematic methods of Richard Wagner, Giuseppe Verdi, and other opera composers who followed.

Mozart's chamber works cover a staggering range of ensembles, far wider than Haydn's or Beethoven's, and too long to list here. On the smaller side are the sonatas for violin and piano, only some of which approach Beethoven's in length and scale, but still boasting many gems; six piano trios, of which No. 6, in E major, is the most popular; two great quartets for piano and strings (violin, viola, and cello); a stupendous Divertimento for String Trio that surely affected Beethoven throughout his career; and an equally remarkable Quintet for Piano and Winds (oboe, clarinet, horn, and bassoon). Beethoven used this as the model for his own Quintet for Piano and Winds in the same key, which we will look at in chapter 7. The Clarinet Quintet of 1789 is incomparable and well-known, but jewel of the Trio for Piano, Viola, and Clarinet (K. 498) is a bit of a sleeper in Mozart's amazingly diverse catalog. Mozart's boldest and most innovative chamber works, however, may be the six quintets he wrote for two violins, two violas, and cello—five of them important—where he breaks ground in sonority, complexity, spaciousness of design, and emotional depth; here again Beethoven designed his String Quintet, Op. 29, on Mozart's model.

As noted above, Mozart composed ten important string quartets out of a total of twenty-three. The first six of the mature works were written after a close study of Haydn's Op. 33 quartets and are dedicated to the older master. Though a generation apart, the two giants developed a close friendship, stirring to consider, with Haydn famously writing to Mozart's father in 1785 that his son was "the greatest composer known to me, either in person or by name." Yet more tantalizing to imagine are the performances in Mozart's apartment of several quartets with Haydn on first violin, the composer Karl Ditters von Dittersdorf on second violin, Mozart on viola, and Johann Baptist Vanhal on cello, forming the all-time all-star string quartet. Mozart's six "Haydn" Quartets, dense and cerebral in conception and execution, served as models for Beethoven, as we'll see. Equally intricate are the final four of Mozart's quartets, with the last two featuring prominent cello parts for the king of Prussia, Friedrich Wilhelm II, who commissioned them.

Advanced though Beethoven's final compositions—the late string quartets—are musically, intellectually, and emotionally, they still display his debt to Haydn and Mozart.

Beethoven's chamber music falls into three tiers of importance, the first level taken up by the five sonatas for cello and piano which we'll look at in chapter 5; the ten sonatas for violin and piano (chapters 3 and 4); the six important piano trios published as Opp. 1, 70, and 97 (chapter 6); and, preeminently, the sixteen string quartets, covered in chapters 8 through 14. Less than crucial but still well worth getting to know are the four string trios, Opp. 3 and 9; the superb but rarely performed String Quintet, Op. 29; the Quintet for Piano and Winds, like Op. 29 also modeled on Mozart; the charming Septet, Op. 20; and the Serenade for String Trio, Op. 8. There's also a fine set of variations for piano trio—known as the "Kakadu" Variations—that's covered in chapter 6 with the other compositions for that ensemble. There's a lower rung of pieces also looked at briefly, with the one-offs, in chapter 7.

Beethoven composed chamber music throughout his career. Some of his earliest efforts are piano quartets; the first pieces he found fit to publish with an opus number (a sequencing of major published works) are the three piano trios, Op. 1, from 1794–95. And he devoted his final years to five late string quartets, Opp. 127, 132, 130, 131, and 135; Op. 133, the *Grosse Fuge*, is for string quartet, and the last composition completed by Beethoven was a new finale for the Op. 130 Quartet. So chamber ensembles occupied him from start to finish, through all the remarkable permutations of his style.

The composer's oeuvre is typically divided into three periods, but four may be more accurate, because there is a transitional phase between the middle and late periods that's probably long and distinctive enough to merit its own number.

Beethoven's early period includes his works up to about 1803; the middle, covers everything he wrote between 1803 and 1817; and the late period starts with the "Hammerklavier" Sonata for Piano, Op. 106, of 1817–18 and lasts until his death in March 1827. Although Beethoven's individual and powerful style is evident in compositions from the early and mid-1790s, his reliance on earlier models, chiefly Haydn, with whom he studied, and Mozart is clearest. The middle period is the phase in which Beethoven's best-known and most popular works, including the Third (nicknamed the "Eroica"), Fifth, and Seventh Symphonies and two of the most popular piano sonatas, the "Waldstein" and the "Appassionata," were conceived. Here Beethoven has expanded the dimensions of his work in every way. The pieces are longer, more complex (and even early Beethoven is far from simple), more dramatic, and even violent. The third period—Beethoven's greatest—is marked by a more inward manner, more "mystical" and more mysterious, too. The late period contains works that are generally but not exclusively enormous in scale. Its most famous manifestation, the Symphony No. 9, is a public work, which speaks in a big way to an audience that is now worldwide. But many of the late compositions, including some that we will look at in this survey, speak with a voice as individual—and sometimes eccentric—and intimate as any music can.

The late works for chamber ensemble are chiefly the five final quartets, but the last Sonata for Violin and Piano, Op. 96, though chronologically earlier (1812), seems to anticipate the composer's late manner, too. The important chamber works of the middle period are the three String Quartets of Op. 59; the "Harp" Quartet, Op. 74; the big Sonata for Cello and Piano, Op. 69; the two Piano Trios of Op. 70; and the final Piano Trio, nicknamed the "Archduke," Op. 97. The three Violin and Piano Sonatas of Op. 30, and the powerful "Kreutzer" Sonata, Op. 47, round out the group. The early ensemble works of highest significance are the six string quartets of Op. 18; the three Piano Trios of Op. 1; the String Trios, Op. 9; the Violin and Piano sonatas, Opp. 12, 23, and 24, the last of which is nicknamed the "Spring" Sonata; and the two Cello and Piano Sonatas of Op. 5. Perhaps the really fine Quintet for Piano and Winds should also be added to the list.

This grouping leaves out three important works: the two cello and piano sonatas of Op. 102 (1815) and the solitary String Quartet in F Minor, Op. 95 (1810), known as the "Serioso." The cello works are thorny examples of the transitional period, anticipating Beethoven's late style, and hard to place into the style of the middle period. The F Minor Quartet, which we will study in chapter 11, is an astonishing work, so individual and concentrated that it's hard to fit it comfortably into *any* of Beethoven's stylistic periods.

Beethoven's works for chamber ensembles, coming from his entire career and for such a wide a range of ensembles, makes it difficult, even foolish, to generalize about this crucial part of his output. But it's safe to say that you can hear in it everything from the fastest, hair-trigger ensemble playing to his most profound utterances. And if you find the whole category overly esoteric, I can only state the obvious: the only way to start is by listening. What's more, you can ease your way in, beginning with the sonatas for piano and violin and then the cello sonatas, in which you'll hear two familiar instruments in dialogue. Then we'll move up to the denser textures of the piano trios, with a look at the string trios along the way. We'll take a detour at some of the less familiar pieces, including the string and wind quintets, and the septet. Only when you've had a chance to digest these will we take look at the string quartets, where the composer works on more challenging ideas. Here the progression from the high-classical formalism of the six Op. 18 quartets through the groundbreaking Op. 59, the aurally lush "Harp" quartet, and the dense "Serioso" is beautiful to trace. Then we'll take on the mighty late quartets; the climb through those peaks should prove one of the most exhilarating passages of your listening life. And even these advanced works offer more in the way of light and air than you might expect.

Beethoven's Life

As the composer whose music is probably the most widely admired, the basic facts of Beethoven's life are well known. And as one learns about Beethoven's pain-filled life and difficult personality, the deafness that overtook him as he reached artistic maturity in his late twenties obviously and inevitably becomes the most striking paradox of his biography. It seems inconceivable that a deaf musician could produce work of such beauty, complexity, and depth—miraculous for us, but of course terrible for the man himself. Beethoven's deafness will always make him the most vivid and heroic composer.

Beethoven was baptized in Bonn, a small German city on the Rhine, on December 17, 1770, and is presumed to have been born on the day before to Johann van Beethoven and his wife, Maria Magdalena. Johann's father, whose name was originally Louis but was later Germanicized to Ludwig, was born in Mechelen, in what is now Belgium, which accounts for the Low Country tang of the "van" in the family name. This Louis/Ludwig was a good singer and keyboard player, as was his son Johann. But neither father nor grandfather displayed talent that anticipated the magnitude of their descendant's, as in the Bach or Mozart families. Maria Magdalena was a Bonn native of deeply serious character whom the composer revered, and from whom he presumably inherited his own earnest manner.

Most of the composer's early musical training was from his father, who was evidently severe, even with a pupil of Beethoven's youth and gifts. He had the child perform in public as early as 1778, apparently in the hope that he would be viewed as a second Mozart, the child prodigy and income machine for his own family in the 1760s. This

Beethoven was not; nor was his father an astute promoter and businessman like Leopold Mozart. But like Mozart, Beethoven was in the public eye from early on. In 1780 or thereabouts he began to study with Christian Gottlob Neefe, a gifted musician who introduced him to Bach's *Well-Tempered Clavier*. It was difficult music to grasp and to play, but it must have stimulated the young Beethoven's imagination. Certainly Beethoven's studies of Bach and Handel can be seen in his ever-deepening commitment to counterpoint, which pays off with the counterpoint-saturated masterworks, including the string quartets, of his late period. (Counterpoint—or polyphony—is the complex, note-against-note compositional technique that for most listeners reached its peak in the music of Bach and Handel; fugue and canon are two well-known contrapuntal processes. Polyphony's opposite number is homophony, in which a strongly profiled melody moves over a subservient accompaniment, as in an operatic aria. Like many composers who followed the polyphonic masters of the Baroque era, Beethoven typically reserved counterpoint for the expression of lofty or serious affects, and as a display of his most advanced compositional skills.)

By 1782 Beethoven had begun composing. Some of his juvenile works included three quartets for piano and strings, much in Mozart's style, but with keyboard parts of notable difficulty, reflecting the composer's own skill as a player. Hoping to study with Mozart, Beethoven left Bonn for Vienna in early 1787. The trip subsidized by Max Franz, the elector, or ruler, of the little principality of which Bonn was the capital. As is typical for a famous artist, a number of legends have been incorporated into Beethoven's biography. Verified facts of Beethoven's first visit to Vienna are few; and although the idea of Mozart praising Beethoven's playing and saying the younger man would "give the world something to talk about" is an appealing one, it's unclear whether Mozart and Beethoven actually met. Beethoven's description of Mozart's playing to his factually reliable pupil Carl Czerny as "fine but choppy, with no legato,"[1] does indicate that he at least heard Mozart play. But Beethoven would have to learn everything he was to absorb from Mozart by studying the music on his own, which he did thoroughly.

Beethoven was recalled prematurely to Bonn by his mother's final illness; she died of tuberculosis in July 1787. With his father sinking into alcoholism, the young Beethoven, known already for his moody, stubborn character, had to assume the dominant role in his family, which included two younger brothers, Johann and Carl. He also resumed his place in Bonn's musical life, playing the viola in the elector's court orchestra. Here he probably participated in performances of music at all levels of quality, up to and including Haydn symphonies and Mozart operas. In 1790 he composed the elevated and ambitious *Cantata on the Death of Emperor Joseph II*—scarce in recordings but well worth hearing—and a slightly less fine cantata to celebrate the coronation of Joseph's successor, Leopold. Haydn saw and praised the score of one of these when passing through Bonn on his way to England. In 1792, on his way back, Haydn and the younger master met again, and it seems likely that Haydn then accepted Beethoven as his pupil, signaling the end of Beethoven's time in his provincial hometown.

In November 1792 Beethoven left Bonn for Vienna to study with Haydn and make his own way as a composer. His friends inscribed a farewell album, in which the brilliant Count Waldstein (to whom the Op. 53 piano sonata is dedicated) wrote, "With unceasing diligence you will receive the spirit of Mozart [who had died in December 1791] from the hands of Haydn,"[2] predicting Beethoven's role as the next practitioner of musical art at its highest level. It didn't take long for Waldstein's prophecy to come true; by 1796 Beethoven was the acknowledged young master of Viennese musical life, with only Haydn as his senior. The traditional view that Beethoven's lessons with Haydn didn't go well owing to Beethoven's impatience now seems to lack nuance. As Barry Cooper points out in his biography,[3] Haydn helped Beethoven by lending him money and arranging for lessons with the highly esteemed contrapuntalist Johann Albrechtsberger before Haydn left for a second tour of England in early 1794. For his part, Beethoven paid for coffee and chocolate for himself and Haydn.

The years leading to and just after 1800 were productive in all ways for Beethoven, who built his reputation as a brilliant pianist and a fiery composer of genius in Vienna's lively musical scene. Performances were typically given either at public concert halls, as pioneered by Mozart, or in the private music salons of the nobility. As a great pianist, Beethoven was sought out by the aristocracy, whose financial support he required

but whom he resented and treated roughly—but then, he treated everyone roughly at times. The typical concerts of the time would shock a
modern listener, for they consisted of movements of concertos and
symphonies, which, even at their premieres, were interspersed with
improvisations, or even arias from popular operas of the day. In any
case, performances by Beethoven remained hot tickets until deafness
ended his career as a pianist.

It used to be a commonplace of Beethoven biographies that he
was the first composer to free himself from the bonds of aristocratic
patronage. In fact, Mozart took the plunge before Beethoven; and
our hero, although in no one's hire, remained dependent on wealthy
and aristocratic patrons. Like Mozart, he resented his position, but
Beethoven was incapable of hiding his resentment. To a great extent,
Beethoven's renowned independence was really a pretense to protect his
touchy pride; thus, dedications of works to the nobility were generally
rewarded with cash gifts of appreciation in return.[4] In a remarkable
instance, a grateful Beethoven dedicated the peerless String Quartet in
C-sharp Minor, Op. 131, to Baron von Stutterheim, whose regiment the
composer's nephew Karl joined in 1826, much to the composer's relief.

But one name—that of the Archduke Rudolph—stands out among
the various barons, counts, and princesses who received dedications of
important works. A member of the Austrian royal family, the son and
brother of Austrian emperors, Rudolph was a very big fish as patrons
went, and a composition student of Beethoven's as well. That Rudolph
selected Beethoven as his teacher demonstrates the composer's preemi-
nence in the Austrian musical universe. Among the works dedicated to
Rudolph are (unsurprisingly) the "Archduke" Trio, Op. 97, which we'll
look at in chapter 6; the Fourth and Fifth Piano Concertos; three piano
sonatas, Opp. 81a (a musical testimony to Beethoven's friendship with
the archduke), 106, and 111; and, to celebrate Rudolph's installation as
archbishop of Olmütz in 1820, the *Missa Solemnis*, although Beethoven
didn't complete the mass until 1822. The mild-mannered Rudolph was
apparently a talented pianist and musician.[5] He was also well suited
temperamentally to study with the excitable Beethoven, who seems in
this one instance to have controlled his temper, probably in view of his
student's rank as well as knowing how much the archduke-archbishop

had done and could do on his behalf. Which, indeed, was considerable: Rudolph was one of three nobles who in 1809 endowed a fund to keep Beethoven in Vienna when Napoleon's brother offered him a job elsewhere. But genuine warmth does appear to have developed between the unlikely pair. Two other important patrons were the Russians Count Andreas Razumovsky, to whom the Op. 59 string quartets were dedicated, and Prince Nikolai Galitzin, who commissioned the first three of the five late quartets.

Beethoven published his first important works, the Piano Trios Op. 1 and the Piano Sonatas Op. 2. The composer always reserved opus numbers for the works he considered most important, though he wrote many others for quick income; as a respected composer, Beethoven was able to sell anything and everything he wrote. But the important works composed in the fertile years of his first period are many and astonishing. Beethoven strove for and achieved mastery in the instrumental genres he inherited from Haydn and Mozart, including the keyboard sonata and concerto, the string quartet (with the six of Op. 18), his sole, neglected string quintet (Op. 29) of 1801, and the symphony, of which the First and Second are magnificent examples of the high-classical style. No such description can be applied to the Third—the "Eroica"—of 1805, with which Beethoven shattered the boundaries of symphonic form and convention to create one of the great disruptive works in music and, indeed, in art.

Even as his productivity and genius surged, Beethoven's greatest personal crisis also reached a climax. In October 1802 Beethoven wrote a document known as the Heiligenstadt Testament, named for the Viennese suburb where it was drafted. Beethoven kept the document, which is actually a letter addressed to his brothers Carl and Johann (though Johann's name is curiously omitted throughout), and it was discovered among his papers after his death in 1827. Beethoven states in the letter that he had been suffering from ringing and buzzing in his ears for six years, which puts the onset of these symptoms back to 1797. Thus it appears almost certain that Beethoven suffered from tinnitus, of which ringing in the ears is the chief symptom. The cause of the illness is unknown, and physicians were of no help. By the spring of 1802 Beethoven's discomfort was so severe that he fled Vienna in a desperate attempt to cure the problem; six months later, no better, and having wrestled with and accepted his fate, he wrote this moving confession. He described his love for humanity, and how his reticence in social situations had been misconstrued as misanthropy; he wrote bitterly of the loss of his hearing, which faculty he had once had in the "highest perfection." And he dedicated himself and the rest of his life to his art.

It's unfathomable that Beethoven's creativity flourished, as though functioning in a different sphere, in spite of his increasing deafness. His productivity remained undiminished, and a look at some of the works he completed in the terrible yet fertile years of 1800, 1801, and 1802 tells a remarkable story: they include the Symphony No. 2; the six Op. 18 quartets; the Sonatas for Piano and Violin Opp. 23, 24, and 30, notable for their high energy and generally high spirits; and the Piano Sonatas Opp. 22, 26, 27, 28, and 31, brilliant works that, with a couple of important exceptions, reflect little in the way of tragic emotion.

On the practical side, Beethoven dealt with his hearing loss in various ways. Some of his pianos were built with amplification plates to magnify their sound. In 1816 the composer began to employ an ear trumpet to try to capture conversations, but by 1818 his hearing had deteriorated so badly that he began to use conversation books. In these, Beethoven's friends and guests wrote questions and comments to which the composer replied verbally. Many concern mundane matters, while others offer tantalizing, one-sided discussions about musical art. Again and again, however, these methods of communication only underline Beethoven's endless isolation. Its most terrible public manifestation, well-known and attested to, took place during the premiere in 1824 of the Ninth Symphony, which Beethoven nominally conducted while the orchestra secretly watched another leader. At the end of the second movement or the finale—it's unclear which—the audience broke into wild applause. Lost in his score, his back to the crowd, Beethoven couldn't hear the tumult; finally one of the singers turned him around to face the cheering crowd.

Deafness was far from Beethoven's only health problem, though it was of course the most crippling. He was prone to digestive and abdominal ailments as well, and died on March 26, 1827, apparently of liver disease, intestinal disease—possibly colitis—and kidney failure at a relatively young fifty-six, old though he looked. He suffered from a variety of illnesses for the last ten years of his life, yet labored on, composing some of his greatest music in the wake of his physical sufferings. The A-flat Major Piano Sonata, Op. 110, of 1821, composed after bouts with rheumatism and jaundice, is a work of profound beauty and a sense of ever-rising strength. The most notable example of his direct musical response to recuperation, from an even more serious illness suffered in 1825, is the sublime slow movement of the A Minor String Quartet, Op. 132, which he subtitled "Holy Song of Thanksgiving to the Deity by a Convalescent, in the Lydian Mode," which we'll examine in chapter 12.

Beethoven's mental health raises other questions. He was difficult even when young, well, and able to hear, and deafness exacerbated his moodiness and paranoid tendencies. Deafness also threw Beethoven's eccentricity into high relief, making it easy for the vulgar to call him crazy. That his music was the most advanced of its day and consequently laden with difficulties allowed some musicians, including fine ones such as the composer Carl Maria von Weber, to question his sanity, too;[6] but it seems to have been widely accepted in the musical community that Beethoven was a pioneer, "composing for the future." And in spite of his often troublesome personality, Beethoven had close friendships to the end: some who knew him well spoke of his high-mindedness and even, remarkably, called him a greater man than artist.[7] Even deaf, Beethoven had charisma and what seems to have been a genuine sweetness, always tempered by bluntness, that held the loyalty of a small inner circle.

Nothing underscores Beethoven's personal awkwardness with greater clarity than his painfully clumsy attempts to dominate the lives of his family. As the oldest of three surviving siblings, he felt free to dictate to his two brothers in all matters, imposing his own genuinely high morals on two average men who chafed under the burden. Carl's marriage to Johanna Reiss in 1806 against Beethoven's wishes, and the composer's litigation to deprive Johanna of her maternal rights after Carl's death in 1815, can be read about in the biographical studies, but the story shows the composer at his most aggressive—although, ironically, his harsh assessment of Johanna's character was on target. Later, Beethoven's smothering love for his nephew Karl drove the poor, ordinary youth back to his mother and finally, in 1826, to attempt suicide. All these events display the composer's lack of emotional moderation, and all may have taken a toll on his physical well-being.

Beethoven had an active, if apparently chaste, love life that has been the subject of endless study and speculation. He loved women, and some were inevitably attracted to him, but he never married and was not a seducer, which his personal morality forbade.[8] He fell in love many times: an early passion was one Magdalena Willman, also from Bonn, to whom he proposed in 1795, presumably in Vienna, but who turned him down "because he was so ugly and half crazy."[9] Many of his loves were aristocrats, just above his station, to whom he taught piano, or were married women. A number of commentators have suggested that the composer was attracted to women who weren't available to him for one reason or another, because he knew that solitude was essential to the fulfillment of his art. It makes sense that he never married because he was too busy to share his life with someone else, but he suffered terribly from loneliness as a result.

In 1812 Beethoven wrote a passionate letter to a woman addressed only as "Immortal Beloved," which was found, unsent like the Heiligenstadt Testament, among his papers after his death. This letter has by itself spawned a whole industry, including books and a film or two, to identify the woman to whom it was addressed, but the best recent scholarship points decisively to Antonie Brentano. This Vienna native returned to her hometown with her husband from Frankfurt between 1809 and 1812, when she and Beethoven would have come to know one another. Brentano is, indeed, one of those who wrote warmly of Beethoven the man. But Beethoven had to renounce her, and the idea of conjugal love. This seems to have been his last serious love, and its end coincides with the start of the six-year drop-off in his output, from 1812 to 1817.

Beethoven did not stop composing during this period; indeed, he wrote many wonderful works over these years. But they are fewer and generally smaller in scale than those of either the immensely fertile period before or the one that would follow starting in 1817. One project he undertook was the revision in 1814 of his opera *Fidelio* into its final form, no small task. And many of the works of the period, while stylistically various—the Piano Sonatas Opp. 90 and 101; the Sonatas for Cello and Piano Op. 102; the Tenth (and last) Sonata for Piano and Violin, Op. 96; and the song cycle *An die ferne Geliebte* (To the Distant Beloved), Op. 98—are hardly insignificant. It is, of course, impossible to know why the master's creative engine downshifted for six years. It would be easy to blame the illness and death of his brother Carl and the composer's subsequent legal battle with Johanna for custody of her and Carl's son, Karl, but Beethoven had always been able to deal with personal business while composing without his productivity suffering in the least. And he continued to deal with the same difficult matters once the tide of inspiration rose again in 1817 with the "Hammerklavier" Sonata, Op. 106, ending the apparent creative drought.

Over the years, Beethoven had developed methods of stimulating his imagination by improvising at the keyboard and, in later years, keeping sketchbooks at hand at all times, even by his bedside, so that he could jot down ideas as they came or work more extensively on material as he took his daily walks. Tales of his humming and howling as he worked through an idea are common in his biographies. And once a work was in process, everything else took second place. Students waited or were dismissed without their lessons and meals were skipped until Beethoven was satisfied that the process had run its course.[10] A young friend's recollection is deeply revealing:

> He was once expected for dinner with us, and it was getting close to two, our dinner-time. My parents feared, with good reason, that he might have got deep into composing and forgotten all about the time, and sent me over to fetch him. I found him at his desk, facing the open door to the piano room, writing one of the last (Galitzin) quartets. He looked up and told me to wait a bit, until he had put his idea down on paper. I was quiet for a while and then went over to the Graf piano (with the added amplifying apparatus), which was nearest, and began to strum lightly on the keys, not being convinced that Beethoven was deaf to musical tones. . . . He heard nothing, and kept on writing, unconcerned, until finally he was finished and came out with me.[11]

While demonstrating the depth of Beethoven's deafness in his last years, Gerhard von Breuning's story shows a methodical artist at work—more disciplined athlete than wild-eyed visionary, even while composing visionary music. Certainly Beethoven suffered in the act of creation, but it also brought him the joy that only creators can know.

The Sonatas for Violin and Piano

Nos. 1–5

Beethoven wrote ten sonatas for violin and piano, the first five of which, covered in this chapter, come from his early period. In terms of style, the description applies well to the first three, which Beethoven composed in 1797–98, and published as his Op. 12. The fourth and fifth sonatas, from 1800 and 1801 and published singly as Opp. 23 and 24, reflect a changing style as the composer moved toward the intensity and expanded scale of his middle-period style. The fifth sonata, nicknamed the "Spring" Sonata, is one of Beethoven's most lyrical chamber works and, along with the Sonata No. 9 for Piano and Violin, Op. 47, nicknamed the "Kreutzer" Sonata, is the most frequently performed of the ten.

The sonata for violin and keyboard accompaniment is likely the most popular chamber ensemble. There are more works for these two instruments than for any other combination, probably because audiences like the sound of the paired instruments, and, more practically, because there are more violinists than players of any other string instrument, and more keyboard players than all other instrumentalists. Beethoven was one of the great pianists of his time, and apparently a decent string player as well, since the viola was his second instrument and the violin his third. From the first sonata through the tenth, the piano part in these works is as important as the violin's, making them meetings of equals, rather than display pieces for the fiddle with piano accompaniment or vice versa; the piano parts throughout the ten are almost as dense and difficult as the piano sonatas. In fact, all of his chamber works with piano have hard keyboard parts, showing Beethoven's personal bond with the instrument.

Bach's sonatas for harpsichord and violin are profound and energetic works that also demand high skill from both players, but it is uncertain whether Beethoven knew them, especially early in his career, when the publication of Bach's music was more hit-or-miss. Works for keyboard and violin from the classical era before Beethoven often featured more difficult parts for the keyboard player, with the violinist adding color to melodic phrases with simple lines of a single note. But Mozart changed that with his sixteen superb sonatas for piano and violin, in which the piano parts are challenging, and the violin parts, if not virtuosic, are expressive and exquisitely balanced with the piano. In the sea of Mozartean masterworks for chamber ensembles, the piano and violin sonatas may even be a bit neglected. While some of Mozart's earlier piano and violin sonatas are relatively modest in scale, the later ones are full-sized sonatas, and it is from these that Beethoven took his cue. Like Mozart and countless other composers, Beethoven here followed the tradition of publishing his works in six or its multiples—usually twelve—or divisors, as in groups of three, like the Opp. 12 and 30 sonatas.

A typical slow movement in one of Mozart's instrumental works will feature an arialike melody over a light accompaniment. Inspired by the Italian (and Viennese) operatic schools of the late eighteenth century, these clear, expressive tunes defined a crossover instrumental style, one based on a vocal ideal that was beyond popular in music of the late eighteenth and early nineteenth centuries. Mozart's effortless handling of the style reflects his mastery of the operatic models. To improve his own less natural abilities in the manner, Beethoven studied vocal composition with Antonio Salieri, the most respected composer of opera in Vienna (and the ostensible villain of Peter Shaffer's highly fictionalized play and film *Amadeus*). As we examine these sonatas and other works in the Beethoven canon, you'll read about many examples of Italianate, arialike, or operatic tunes; it is to this style that I'll be referring.

All three of the compositions that make up Op. 12 adhere to the standard classical-era format of three movements, with the first and last in quick tempos and the middle movement in a slower one. Seven of Beethoven's ten in this category have three movements; the other three (Op. 24, Op. 30 No. 3, and Op. 96) have four, the additional movement being a scherzo, a character piece in a quick tempo that Beethoven places third in the sequence of four. Other early-period instrumental works, including one of the Op. 18 string quartets and a number of the piano sonatas, feature a minuet in the same spot, an abstract descendant of a well-known courtly dance of the eighteenth century. The large-scale scherzo is Beethoven's own creation, with Mozart and Haydn invariably placing a minuet (using its Italian name, *menuetto*) third in a four-movement work. We'll examine Beethoven's scherzos individually as we look at each work, but where the minuet is graceful and dignified, Beethoven's scherzos are playful, punchy, and sometimes violent.

Although the Sonata in D Major, Op. 12 No. 1, has the least distinctive personality of the Op. 12 works, it is a fine specimen of the high-classical ensemble piece, providing a good X-ray of Beethoven's structural procedures. The first movement is in what's known as *sonata form*. This structure involves a three-part movement. First is the *exposition*, in which the themes are set out (usually there are two or three); then comes the *development*, in which the themes are taken apart, blended, and put through a few harmonic changes. Finally we get the *recapitulation*, which restates the opening material, although rarely in precisely the same manner as at the beginning. There may also be a *coda*, a closing section with some rhetorical emphasis. Most sonata-form movements by Haydn and Mozart end plainly, without codas, as do Beethoven's in his early period. But Beethoven took to writing longer and more important codas over his career, with some later ones, as in the Third and Fifth Symphonies, taking on gargantuan dimensions and force.

The work opens with a ceremonious flourish typical of the period, energetic in rhythm but of no particular melodic distinction and played by both instruments. A suave and somewhat more memorable tune follows in the violin, with the piano providing accompaniment with a steady flow of eighth notes. When you listen, note how closely the two instruments' parts are blended, because this will be a feature of all Beethoven's chamber sonatas, and, indeed, all his works for chamber ensembles. The third element in the opening subject is a busy, spinning phrase, followed by scales and turns. It's common for sonata subjects to include several thematic ideas, as Beethoven offers us here, and often we will chiefly be looking at *subject groups* like this rather than single melodies or themes. The second theme, more relaxed and lyrical, enters in graceful falling eighth notes before moving into a more energetic section featuring triplets, the pulsing, slightly breathless decorative device where three notes are played in the space that would otherwise be occupied by two. The third thematic group, which opens with a vigorous chord sequence played by both instruments, serves as the exposition's closing idea, rounding out the cast of thematic characters.

Beethoven uses this chordal group to open the brief development section, which roams through some minor keys, darkening the tone of the music. Steering toward the recapitulation, Beethoven brings back the opening flourish, which the piano plays quietly, under an even stream of notes in the fiddle. A long trill, first taken up by the piano, then picked up by the violin, brings back the closing theme, which concludes the movement. Again, the sharing of ideas, long and short, and their constant exchange between the players is a feature of this sonata, as in all of the composer's chamber works to come.

Beethoven uses the variation form for the second movement. Perhaps the title is self-explanatory, but specifically it's a theme, stated at the beginning, subjected to several permutations, each of a different character. Variations were popular in European music; as we'll see, the form took on growing importance in Beethoven's thought. This set, on an amiable two-part theme in a moderate tempo, is not among his major efforts in this form. The first of the four variations races in quicker notes, with piano having the more ornate part. The second variation moves in a graceful, dancelike rhythm, the piano stating the melody and the violin adding commentary. The stormy third variation, in A minor (the theme and other variations are in A major), is surely the most memorable. Here, Beethoven reduces the theme to its barest profile over menacing rumblings from the piano and powerful chords for the violin. In the fourth and final variation, Beethoven returns to A major for a tender dialogue in which both instruments play in a throbbing, syncopated rhythm. And as is typical of him, Beethoven adds a delicate little coda, breaking the theme into falling triplets, that actually forms another variation.

The third and most interesting movement of this sonata is a rondo, one of the most useful forms for instrumental finales to composers of the classical period. On paper, the rondo is straightforward, with a recurring main theme alternating with individual episodes, so that a rondo with three episodes is laid out as ABACADA, with A as the main theme and the other letters as the episodes; but Beethoven, like Haydn and Mozart, found ways to enrich it, blending it with sonata form by adding development sections or by bringing episodes back. Again, we'll look at each on its own, but typically the rondo's character tends toward the playful, and as Beethoven placed more and more weight on his finales he used other structures, including sonata form and variation, as well as rondo hybrids to carry the load. This is a typical frisky classical rondo on a theme with a joyous, skipping rhythm. The first episode, in a complementary pulse, also contains a thoughtful pause. The return of the main theme contains a surprising and fine shift to D minor; the second episode, in a broader rhythm and with yet another surprising change of key, is more tranquil. Even here, Beethoven tinkers with form—the third episode essentially reprises the first—and a coda featuring alternations of soft and loud passages ends the work.

In place of the generic material that opens this first sonata in the group, Op. 12 No. 2, in A major, is bursting with personality. Haydn's spirit can be heard in the opening theme, more of a motto than a full-flown melody. The piano plays this fragmentary melodic element, which rises as it falls, while the violin comically plays a chuckling rhythmic accompaniment, reversing the normal roles of the instruments. At once graceful and witty—much in Haydn's manner—this marvelous theme dominates the movement. The second theme moves in a steadier, long–short pulse, and a long silence enters as part of the texture and provides an amusing effect. The closing idea, even smoother in its rhythmic profile but mysteriously harmonized, elegantly pulls everything together with its broader pulse. Pay attention when you listen to the very tight exchanges of thematic material from piano to violin and back, with the two instruments acting almost as one. Beethoven scrambles his material conventionally in the short development section. In the recapitulation, however, the composer expands his themes, ending the movement with a short, funny coda that strips the opening theme down in a Haydnesque way to an unemphatic and surprising ending.

Like that of its predecessor, the tempo of the A Major Sonata's second movement is not really slow. But its stately procession of melancholy thematic material could hardly differ more from the swiftly flowing comedy of the first movement. Here the piano kicks off a series of ideas in various pulsing rhythms, in which it is soon joined by the violin in a tightly woven dialogue. As for its form, the movement is in three parts, with the third repeating the material of the first and the middle section offering a strong contrast in the way of flowing scales, first from the violin and then from the keyboard, in a more conciliatory tone. This form is known by the shorthand ABA, with the similar material of the outer sections represented by the A's and the contrasting middle by the B; it's probably the most common form for slow movements in the classical era. When the opening ideas return, Beethoven restates them with more emphasis, so that everything sounds more somber, more desolate, and more angry.

The third movement is an elegant rondo in a playful mood that complements the first movement and contrasts as strongly as possible with the second. There are two beautiful episodes, and Beethoven's skill at making much music from the barest thematic fragments can be heard in the long-short-short rhythmic figure with which he initially links the sections, then uses disruptively later. Note also the comical Haydnesque ending, in which Beethoven displaces the parts: the violin ends first, leaving the piano to finish alone on an empty, hanging phrase.

Haydn's influence is also clear in the third, and probably finest, of the three Op. 12 sonatas, in E-flat major. The first movement states a graceful theme that sweeps over the keyboard, closely tracked by the violin. However, the thematic elements that follow are fraught with a nervous energy expressed in swirls of rapid notes and wiggling figures that have much in common with the style of Beethoven's great teacher, and the second theme is more mellow and thoughtful, much in the vein of Haydn's so-called popular style. (This describes Haydn's manner of adapting of folk and popular music into the works of his maturity, from about 1790 to his death in 1809.)[1] The closing group brings back nervous blizzards of notes and three explosive outbursts that are pure

Beethoven. Throughout, hair-trigger coordination is needed to bring off this technically difficult movement. The stormy development features harsh chords for the violin over busy figuration for the piano, and a striking passage in which the violin plays falling thematic fragments in a faraway key over a trembling accompaniment in the piano seems to take the expression to an altogether higher plane. Beethoven adds a substantial coda to this exceptional sonata movement.

Unlike its Op. 12 companions, this sonata has a middle movement of considerable proportions and depth that's also genuinely slow. A self-consciously sublime melody in the style of an operatic aria, first stated by the piano, features structural elements that Beethoven exploits in various ways over the course of this long adagio. In an interesting passage that follows the opening sequence, the violin sings out the melody, while the piano plays a throbbing accompaniment with a quasi-orchestral texture. In the middle section of this three-part (ABA, as you recall) movement, the violin raptly restates the falling intervals of the opening melody over harplike (arpeggiated) accompaniment by the piano. The swift key changes that mark the long, elaborate closing passage also seem strongly reminiscent of Haydn's style. The closing rondo opens with a sturdy, rustic dance tune but soon soars higher before dissolving into a more vehement phrase; the bewitching closing phrase jumps swiftly between keys. The second episode can be identified by some comically bland fiddling of repeated notes over scales by the piano, but here Beethoven introduces stronger accents and startling key changes that seem more serious. And the closing section (in this movement, the coda) features some polyphonic moments before the mood lightens for the final measures.

Unusual in form and content, the Sonata No. 4 in A Minor, Op. 23, is a transitional work of 1800 with a strong personality. But that personality, by turns cool and fierce, makes it one of the less approachable and popular of this series—a shame, because it's an outstanding work. The two outer movements fly by at very rapid tempos: Beethoven marks the opening movement *presto*. The fluid opening ideas generally share a contained quality, at least until they erupt into angry outbursts. The dour second theme can be recognized by its lilting rhythm. The development section continues in the laconic mood of the exposition, with the opening theme developed into a new, longer melody. The recapitulation offers the second theme in a consoling major-key incarnation, but this is very brief, and the movement ends quite strikingly on an outburst followed by an abrupt and surprising drop in volume for the final chords. The two instruments play in very tight ensemble throughout.

The most unusual movement in the sonata must be the second, which has an interesting tempo marking (*Andante scherzoso, più Allegretto*) that is not truly slow and, with the word *scherzoso* (meaning "jokingly"), suggests playfulness. The opening theme, set forth at first by the piano, sounds like it's made for variations, but instead a second theme, in a *fugato* (fuguelike) character, appears. But instead of developing a fugue, Beethoven now introduces a temporizing, lyrical theme that amusingly goes nowhere. A stormy rondo in a quick tempo concludes the work. The main theme, intense and pressing, is interspersed with three episodes of varying character; the second and longest is an arching lyrical melody for the violin over a calm accompaniment by the piano. The third appearance of the main theme shows Beethoven's characteristic power, with massive chords for the violin over a thunderous running figuration for the keyboard. (The violin has four strings, widely separated in pitch. Four-note chords like these combine stress with power; Beethoven will use this sound to devastating effect in the first movement of the "Kreutzer" Sonata of 1803.) To unify this great work the composer ends this rondo like the opening movement, with a coordinated drop in pitch and volume.

The companion and complement to the tight and dramatic Op. 23 is the "Spring" Sonata—No. 5 in F Major, Op. 24, completed in 1801. The temperaments of these two works could hardly differ more; the F Major Sonata is spacious, mostly relaxed and lyrical. Whereas Op. 23 is relatively obscure, at least in terms of Beethoven's output, the "Spring" is well-known and much beloved. Beethoven sculpts the first theme of the opening allegro movement in such a way as to penetrate the mind: two turns followed by a huge expansion of the phrase into an opulent melody sung by the violin, with the piano quietly accompanying. It dominates the entire movement and sets the mood for the whole piece. (Turns—little figures of rapidly spinning notes—are part of the opening ideas of all three Op. 30 sonatas as well as this one.) The contrasting second theme consists of briskly rising chords for the piano with a repeated-note figure for the violin that opens into several closely related ideas; the closing theme begins with running scales for the fiddle over a walking accompaniment for the keyboard. The short development, in which the composer mixes thematic fragments and runs them through several minor keys, features pulsing triplets as well. The piano states the big opening melody at the start of the recapitulation, which also features several richly expanded versions of the important thematic material. Beethoven ends the movement with a long coda in which he brings back the triplets from earlier in the movement, also extending a phrase from the primary tune to swell with high emotion.

Beethoven employs the aria style for the second movement, a sweet adagio with an operatically styled melody. Several of his contemporaneous piano sonatas feature movements like this. Beethoven at this point is his career is typically dense and earnest where Mozart would be graceful; interestingly, the piano states all the thematic material, which the violin decorates. Rapidly quivering notes mark the tranquil coda.

Beethoven adds a quicksilver scherzo, occupying about one minute's playing time, to create a four-movement format for this sonata. Based on a rhythmic hiccup in the outer parts, the middle section is memorable for its race between the two instruments. The lyrical closing rondo, large in scale, balances the opening movement. This charming but nevertheless substantial movement has two episodes that present a troubled facade, but the storminess is feigned rather than genuine. You'll hear a wailing phrase in which the violin seems to complain; this is followed at once by a cheerful response, with deep rumbling in the piano's lower register. Note how the composer packs this little phrase with shimmering, rapid shifts of key. Pay attention when you listen to how the violin decorates the second return of the main theme with smooth, evenly rising and falling notes, then *pizzicato* (plucked) notes.

The Sonatas for Violin and Piano
Nos. 6–10

In some ways, the combination of violin and piano is a curious one. The instruments themselves could hardly be more different. The little violin can make a huge sound, holding its own against a thundering piano or orchestra, yet it can sing a melody in a way that closely tracks the capabilities of human voice; for flexibility, however, it surpasses the voice and probably all other instruments as well. Think, for instance of how it can scamper from its highest notes to the lowest, and of the range of tones it can produce, from full-throated singing, to plucked, to the silvery whistling timbre known as harmonic. The source of all this sonic magic is a mysteriously resonant, often very beautiful, hollow box of thin lacquered spruce and maple, with a maple neck attached, and four strings that rest on a bridge and are attached to pegs on a head, from which the instrument is tuned—the whole of course played with a wooden bow fitted with a horsehair ribbon that, when brushed across the strings, creates the sound. The fiddle is only about twenty-three inches long. Its chief limitation is its high soprano range, only from middle to very high notes, more than three octaves above, with its lowest note only the G below middle C on a piano (take a look at a keyboard).

Next to the almost mystical simplicity of the violin, the piano is a clunky, elaborate machine. Although often classed as a keyboard, like the organ and harpsichord, it is technically a percussion instrument—the sound is produced by hammers hitting strings—and much of what musicians ask it to do is, paradoxically, sing like a violin, a horn, or a person. Yet, through the artifice of the *sostenuto* (sustain) pedal and in the hands of a good player, it can perform this task surprisingly well;

and, of course, it can carry many other musical functions, too. Its range from low notes to high is enormous—six and one-half octaves—and, in its percussive mode, it can play louder than just about any other instrument. The challenge in composing for these two instruments is to balance their two very different sounds and capabilities and make them play off each other, like (for example) a good comedy team. As you listen and get to know these ten sonatas, you will hear a continual interplay between the piano and violin, with the instruments exchanging thematic elements in close succession. Thus you might hear the violin imitating something that the piano just played deep in its bass. Depending on the effect Beethoven wants, the fiddle might sound the phrase high up or in its lowest range. Eventually you'll start to grasp the concept of ensemble—how the two instruments act together, not as one, but in an intimate discussion. Understanding the concept of ensemble is a key to the appreciation of chamber music in all its forms.

Beethoven composed the three Sonatas for Violin and Piano, Op. 30, in 1802 as he was undergoing a crisis over his deteriorating hearing. It is almost impossible to find in them a trace of despair, though the second sonata, in C minor, is dramatic. Indeed, all display high energy, and the third, in G major, showcases the composer's wild humor.

Beethoven opens the set with the Sonata No. 6 in A Major, a deeply lyrical piece that seems underappreciated. The piano states the tranquil opening theme, which, like all the Op. 30 sonatas, includes a turn, this one calm. The violin adds quiet chords and even notes that sound almost like breathing. The second thematic element is stated by the piano in a more energetic rhythm that differs from the rather broad triple meter, to which Beethoven quickly returns. The second theme, also richly melodious, soon enters to a more active accompaniment (listen for the triplets in the piano), finishing with a busy Haydnesque closing group. The development contains an effective passage in the contrapuntal form called a canon; its closing bars also have a hesitant passage where piano and violin exchange quiet, single notes and chords that are again reminiscent of breathing. You'll notice as you listen that Beethoven assigns the busier material to the piano, with the violin adding a generally calm commentary to this beautiful movement.

The slow movement is, somewhat unusually, a rondo. The violin sings a heart-easing melody over a rocking accompaniment by the piano. In the first episode, the piano sings as the violin takes on the accompaniment; in the second episode, the violin spins out a long, sad melody over a flowing accompaniment by the piano; the third return of the main theme is marked by triplets in place of the rocking figure. The long coda refers once more to the opening phrases, and the movement ends on a graceful dying fall for both instruments.

It appears that Beethoven initially intended the finale that now belongs to the "Kreutzer" Sonata, also in A major, to conclude this work, but found its bounding energy didn't fit the contemplative nature of the first two movements, and so he composed the very beautiful theme and variations that stands as its finale. The melodious two-part theme has a folklike lilt and is quite memorable. In the first of the six variations that follow, the piano and violin trade scurrying triplets; in the suave second variation, the composer spins the melody out into a longer line. The third variation is a *fugato*, a fuguelike passage, usually a serious business for Beethoven. Although the writing for both instruments (note the running bass in the piano) is brilliant and difficult, spirits are high. The instruments play in very different moods, or affects, at the start of the fourth variation: the violin plays big, strong chords as the piano plays in a more abstracted vein, though in the second half it too picks up the chordal idea. The fifth variation, which opens again in contrapuntal style, is long and rather free, breaking into speechlike patterns reminiscent of the contemporaneous "Tempest" Sonata for Piano, Op. 31 No. 2. The sixth variation moves with an almost weightless, dancelike grace to a lyrical, joy-filled coda.

The key mentioned in the title of a musical composition is its tonal home base. Their names—A-flat major, B minor, F major, and so on, through the most common twenty-four—refers to a series of tones that are used repeatedly through the course of the piece. Classical-era compositions typically begin and end unambiguously in their home keys, which also exert a constant gravitational pull over the harmony. While it's unwise to generalize about the moods the keys may imply, it's fair to say that our ears perceive major keys as bright or cheerful, while minor keys are dark and sad. But this shouldn't be taken too literally, because like other great composers Beethoven employed keys with complete freedom, knowing quite well how to make a minor key sound happy and a major one tragic, too. There is no doubt that C minor was Beethoven's signature key, especially in his early and middle periods, when he used it repeatedly to express stress and conflict. Preeminent among the master's important works in C minor is the Symphony No. 5, Op. 67; other important C minor compositions include the Piano Concerto No. 3, Op. 37; and two piano sonatas, the Op. 10 No. 2 and the famous "Pathétique," Op. 13. (One late-period work, the final piano sonata, Op. 111, begins in C minor but ends in an otherworldly C major.) The String Quartet Op. 18 No. 4 is in C minor, as is the next Sonata for Piano and Violin, Op. 32 No. 3. And it's a fine example of Beethoven's use of the key at this stage in his development.

The piano quietly states the tense first theme, a long note followed by a turn and a short note, then a long pause and a reiteration of the opening phrase; then come a menacing, downward-sliding figure and three somber chords. The violin joins in, with the piano adding deep, rumbling accompaniments below. The violin responds to thick chords from the piano with big, fierce chords of its own; the emotional atmosphere Beethoven establishes in about thirty seconds is dramatic and conflict driven. The second theme, given by the violin, is lighter in texture. It's a marchlike figure (long-short-long) over a trotting rhythm in the keyboard accompaniment. March rhythms are remarkably common in the music of the era, reflecting perhaps the omnipresence of armies in that age of the Napoleonic Wars. Mozart knew how to turn them into playful or grand themes, but Beethoven's application here seems almost theatrical, as though a new character has entered the drama. The opening group ends with highly rhetorical figures for both instruments, with the violin jumping from high notes to low and back again, playing big chords over thundering notes and long, surging scales in the piano.

A normal classical exposition would now be repeated; but Beethoven does not want to slow the impetus of this headlong movement, so he plunges directly into a long development section having the character of a battle between thematic elements. The recapitulation is also long, with prominence given to a boiling, passionate phrase from the closing group and a mock-fugal development of the second theme. A long, ferocious coda ends this remarkable movement, an excellent example of Beethoven's growing ability to build a big musical structure from short thematic elements of no great melodic distinction, and of his skill in managing sonata structure to powerful dramatic ends.

Beethoven provides a few minutes of repose in the beautiful slow movement, which is a relatively tranquil Adagio cantabile—the marking means "slow but flowing and songful." As in the first movement, the piano presents the main theme, beautifully sculpted and richly harmonized. The middle section of this three-part structure features a dialogue between the two instruments in which long tones are contrasted against faster rising figuration. Yet the composer has a surprise in store: as the opening theme meanders along in elaborately decorated guise in the return of the first section, two rapid, startling scales by the piano interrupt, as if referring to something outside of the movement. And then, as though nothing happened, the composer guides the movement to its expected end, with some particularly nice pizzicato chords for the violin set against the piano's delicate running figuration. And the meaning of the interruptions? You'll have to decide for yourself.

The joke on which the kaleidoscopic scherzo is based is the almost constant difference in rhythm and emphasis between the two instruments, placing the composer's metric inventiveness on display. When one instrument plays loud the other is soft, and when the piano is banging the violin is sighing or spitting out delicate repeated notes. Beethoven throws in a few more rhythmic distortions, especially in the second half of the sweeping trio (the scherzo's middle section).

The finale is one of the most serious and exciting movements in the piano and violin sonatas. It's in sonata form, which Beethoven used whenever he wanted to express conflict, as he does quite emphatically here. The piano states the curt initial theme, opening with a twisting, six-note figure ripe for development deep in the bass; this then rises to chords that hold some unexpected harmonic changes. A pleading melody in the violin serves as the second element in the opening group, and a transitional passage based on the all-powerful opening figure leads to the spiky second theme, in E-flat major, which seems hardly less tense or vehement. A yearning closing theme rounds out the initial presentation. As in the opening movement, Beethoven forgoes a repeat of the exposition, and for the same reason: to maintain the forward motion of this musical drama. The long coda is fierce and fast, and to the end the work holds uncompromisingly to its grim C minor mood.

The third and last sonata in the Op. 30 set is a miraculous three-movement work in G major. Its high spirits contrast strikingly with the anger and violence of the preceding sonata. It's astonishing to realize that Beethoven composed this joyful music while suffering increasingly from the tinnitus that would destroy his hearing, as well as the torment of accepting his fate. The work also displays his enormous energy.

The sonata's first movement (CD Track 1) opens, like its three predecessors, with a turn, here transformed into a wild, spinning figure for both instruments that then hurtles upward; the second phrase of the opening theme, stated by the piano (0:11), is more tranquil, but the high energy of the opening soon returns. The score contains many notes Beethoven indicates should be accented—at 0:25, 0:28, 0:31, and innumerable other times over the course of the movement, acting as one of its main elements and adding to the already high level of energy with a steady stream of bracing jolts. A beautiful transitional phrase (0:43) leads to the second subject, leaping upward in mock fury (1:03) but spending itself quickly over the ensuing bars. Trills dominate the closing group (staring at 1:47), in which the vigor of the opening returns. The exposition is repeated, as Beethoven instructs (2:00–3:56).

The development, short but aggressive, begins with the violin and piano trading the trills that concluded the opening group (3:57), here sounding more menacing, then passing the opening figure to the piano in its lowest register (4:14), and finally swapping it through different keys and instrumental registers. The recapitulation, which begins quite unmistakably at 4:28, hardly differs from the initial presentation of the thematic material, and Beethoven winds down the volume at the movement's end.

Instead of a reflective adagio, a leisurely and spacious minuet is used as the second movement. Here Beethoven clearly displays the influence of Haydn—especially as the composer of the piano trios, in which the richest fantasy is given free rein. The themes are relaxed and gracious, and Beethoven uses triplets as a means of rhythmic and melodic elaboration; they add an easy pulse while also providing Beethoven space to embroider his thematic material. As the music moves easily toward its conclusion, Beethoven breaks its presentation apart between piano and violin. The finale, a study in perpetual motion, is also richly comical in spirit, with innumerable distortions of rhythm, volume, and, toward the end, key. The themes are all rustic in character, and the violinist has to do some mock country fiddling to conclude this brilliant and flawless sonata.

One of the seminal compositions of the master's middle period, the Sonata No. 9 in A Major, Op. 47, nicknamed the "Kreutzer," is the most famous of Beethoven's ten for piano and violin. The "Kreutzer" is named for a violinist who in fact disliked the composer's work. The original dedicatee, another fiddler named George Bridgetower, premiered the sonata in Vienna in 1803, but after he and Beethoven quarreled, the composer changed his dedication. The sonata is composed in a *concertante* style, "like a concerto."[1] By referring to the concerto style, Beethoven was describing music that's performed by a virtuoso before an audience rather than anything that can be played at home by amateurs. Indeed, both the violin and the piano parts in the "Kreutzer" are extremely difficult.

Although large, the second and third movements may be compared in style and dimension to their opposite numbers in the Op. 30 works. But the titanic first movement is grander in scale and packs a punch far greater than any of its predecessors. Dramatic, majestic, and fierce, any decent performance will leave the listener shaken at the very least; the sensitive newbie may find its violent extremes of tempo, tone, tonality, and dynamics more than he or she can bear. So bold is its power that Tolstoy used the movement as a motivator in his short story "The Kreutzer Sonata." In it, his protagonist feels liberated by its power to act without restraint—in this case, to kill his wife, whom he suspects of having an affair.

Beethoven unifies the immense work with frequent subliminal references to the falling phrase for the violin that opens the sonata. His management of the material ranges from the tight piano reply to the violin's opening chords, through broader reflections on the falling interval in the luxurious closing passage of the second movement, to the second theme of the finale, which is itself a recasting of the opening idea, different though its rhythmic garb makes it appear. And so huge is the first movement that three big thematic groups are needed to carry it.

The sonata opens with a slow introduction, started by huge chords for the violin alone that are echoed and answered by the piano. Even in this A major passage, the harmony twists away from the opening key. The music begins to move in exchanges of fluid passagework between the instruments as the harmony pulls majestically toward A minor, the primary key of the movement; pay attention, too, to the little half-step figure the instruments swap, because two of the movement's main themes are based on it. In fact, the first theme springs directly from the two-note motive. Incisive, fast in tempo, and fiery in character, it differs completely from the meditative affect of the opening passage. Almost immediately, though, Beethoven works in a startling slowdown, the first of many brooding pauses that permeate the music with growing effect as the movement progresses. The theme resumes, only to be interrupted almost at once by a grandiose flourish in the piano; this leads to a long but powerful transitional passage in which the instruments trade driving eighth-note figures, to which the violin occasionally adds trills and big chords. These introduce the most lyrical element of the movement: a second theme consisting of a sculpted melody in long-held notes that shifts regularly and uneasily between E major and E minor. At its end, Beethoven inserts another reduction of tempo in a kind of pause, at once dramatic and reflective, that adds mystery to the movement's vast and volatile emotional palette.

The transitional passage returns, this time so that the piano may introduce the noble third theme, beginning with the half-step interval in a powerful rowing rhythm (short-*long*) that soon broadens majestically; the violin adds lordly commentary in huge pizzicato chords. Beethoven omits the lyrical theme from the long and very difficult development section, in which the first and third themes struggle against the racing transitional material through constantly shifting harmonies; yet another slowdown signals the end of the section and the start of the recapitulation, which again is laden with somber chords—*ritardando*, or slowed down—for the piano. In keeping with the outsized dimensions of the movement, Beethoven endows this passage with what is virtually a second development section. A stormy coda notable for its cathartic climax is interrupted by one last chilling slowdown; this leads to the closing bars, with the racing scales and hammer-blow chords that nail the movement shut.

Beethoven follows this epic drama with a profoundly lyrical theme and, nominally at least, four expansive variations in F major. The two-part theme, very reminiscent of others Beethoven wrote for piano variations around the same time (such as the first movement of his Piano Sonata No. 12, Op. 26, of 1800 and the Variations on an Original Theme, Op. 34, from 1802), is memorable and singable, with perhaps a hint of folksong. It's introduced by the piano, which after the initial statement is joined by the violin. The theme is lavishly decorated by trills, first in the piano and later in the violin. In the first variation the piano renders the theme in dainty separated notes, playfully imitating a string pizzicato, while the violin decorates high above in repeated notes that add great rhythmic character. The second variation gives the violin primacy as it continues the repeated notes of the first but in an uninterrupted stream, moving into very high registers. The third, in F minor, provides a completely different texture as the instruments play *legato*—smoothly tied notes—in a calm, even pace and serious mood. When you listen, note the sad sighs exhaled by the violin at the end of each section. The Mozartean fourth variation, of uncanny delicacy, breaks the theme into dainty runs, trills, and pizzicati for the violin. Its ecstatic tone and glistening sound world anticipate Beethoven's late style, notably the variation movements that end the piano sonatas Opp. 109 and 111 and those in the string quartets Opp. 127 and 131. A very slow, quasi-improvisatory passage leads to one more meditation on the theme, essentially a fifth variation that also serves as a long, reflective, and very beautiful coda. It's entirely typical of Beethoven to toss in a generously proportioned final variation, a tendency that grows more pronounced over his career.

You may remember that the "Kreutzer"'s finale was originally composed for his other violin sonata in the same key, Op. 30 No. 1. But it fits far better in the context of this powerful work than in that of its lyrical predecessor; and it is ironic that Beethoven supplied the astonishing first and second movements to go along with this finale. It's a wild tarantella in sonata form, opening with a thunderous A major chord followed by a procession of tunes in the familiar prancing rhythm of the Italian dance. Stabbing notes provide unceasing rhythmic energy, but the second subject, in a different time signature (2/4), is calm and offers a startling contrast to the wild main theme group. The development takes the material into some dark keys, but of course Beethoven ultimately finds his way back to its original outlines. The coda has some slowdowns for a final iteration of the second theme that recall the ritards—the slowdowns—of the first movement, though here the rhythmic fury of the theme sweeps all before it. Even though written for another work, the movement provides the release of energy this extraordinary composition demands as its conclusion.

Beethoven completed the tenth and last violin and piano sonata in 1812 but did not publish the work until 1816, and he may have revised it before publication. Although it belongs chronologically to the later stage of the master's middle period, many who know this extraordinary work hear in it a forerunner or perhaps even an early example of his late style. In tone it displays the melting sweetness and profound lyricism of the late period, while structurally its trill-laden texture and its finale, a set of variations featuring important contrapuntal passages, are all typical of the late manner. Indeed, apart from the instrumental combination, the Sonata No. 10 in G Major, Op. 96, has little in common with its epic, violent, and athletic predecessor, the "Kreutzer" Sonata. Instead, Op. 96 is almost unfailingly gentle, with a melancholy undertow and hardly a rough edge.

The first movement's opening phrase consists of six long trills, passed in an intimate dialogue between the piano and violin, that swell out into a succession of ecstatic rising and falling eighth notes. A calm second melodic element, in steady repeated eighth notes, may remind you of the pulsating opening of the Piano Concerto No. 4, Op. 58, also in G major. A rumbling transitional phrase introduces triplets into the texture, and they remain integral from this point on. The exquisite second theme, in an unmistakable dance rhythm, is introduced by the piano, with the violin adding quiet triplets. The closing theme is notable for an immensely long (nine-measure) trill for the piano. The development, with a change of key, darkens the tone as Beethoven breaks the phrases of the closing group apart, giving the violin repeated sighing motifs over triplets for piano. In the recapitulation Beethoven allows his already spacious material more and more breathing room, expanding it with exquisite repetitions of phrases in new keys—a typical procedure for him. But here he seems to treat his themes with particular tenderness, as though he can't let them go. The piano repeats the ecstatic nine-bar trill, and in the coda it's shared, slightly abbreviated, by the two instruments.

Unusual in form, the second movement opens with a solemn, hymnlike melody, sung in rich harmony by the piano. The violin enters with a falling three-note figure that pervades this movement, as well as a number of others by the composer.[2] It's essentially the same as the one that famously opens the Piano Sonata in E-flat Major, Op. 81a, nicknamed "Les Adieux"—the farewells—and its meaning here also sounds valedictory. The violin continues with a long, sad melody over a hesitant rhythmic accompaniment by the piano. Soon, however, the violin plays two cadenzas—long, difficult passages with a lot of fast notes that nonetheless maintain the sad affect. These are uncommon in movements of this sort, though, which typically develop in a more regular ABA pattern. The cadenzas finally lead to a return of the main melody, now sung by the violin. The piano plays the "farewell" motif, beginning the long coda in a twilit harmony, with the instruments exchanging long flourishes. A rumble by the piano and an open-ended shift in harmony by the violin signals the end of the movement and the beginning of the scherzo, which follows without pause.

The short scherzo, surely the most sardonic movement in this lyrical work, is set in G minor, the "dark" twin of the rest of the sonata's G major. Even so, it's far from being Beethoven's toughest scherzo. The composer gives the somewhat edgy main theme a tendency toward accents off the expected beat, which may disturb one listener but tickle another. The trio is a beautiful waltz in C major, in which the violin soars high, anticipating some effects in the scherzo of the Op. 135 string quartet (CD Track 12). Beethoven also introduces a brief canon—a tightly imitative passage—into the proceedings. The brief return of the main section is in G minor, but soon there is a shift to G major in preparation for the last movement. When you listen, note the long trill for the violin at the end.

The last movement consists of a three-part theme and about seven variations—it's hard to count them precisely, as we'll see, and Beethoven doesn't number them in the score. The memorable theme has a folklike lilt, similar to what could be heard in Viennese operettas of the day. But the composer adds an almost constant flow of harmonic shadings that put it into a different class and never stop enchanting the listener. Another interesting structural feature of the movement is that Beethoven merges the end of each variation with the beginning of the one that follows. The first variation is a suavely mannered version in which Beethoven compresses the original rhythm. In the second, a more playful incarnation, the piano bustles along under a steady figure for the violin; in the third, the pianist's left hand maintains the momentum as the right hand and the fiddle add melodic and harmonic commentary. In the fourth variation, brisk chords alternate with suave passagework. Suddenly Beethoven slows matters down considerably for the fifth variation, an adagio meditation that contains a few embryonic variations, all set forth articulately amid a welter of trills and a pair of big cadenzas not dissimilar to those in the slow movement, as well as a short reminiscence of the original theme. The busy sixth variation bursts forth in racing sixteenth notes for the piano and perhaps a bit of the vivacity and clear textures of a Bach chorale prelude. Beethoven turns serious in the seventh variation, a canon in G minor that starts the piano's deep notes. The coda, which emerges mysteriously from the end of the canon, may well be regarded as an eighth variation, because even though Beethoven begins it with the main theme, he adds a faster-moving piano part, embellishes the theme considerably, and slows everything down for one more reflective moment just before the joyous closing bars.

The Sonatas for Cello and Piano

I f you were drawing analogies between string instruments and the human voice, the violin would be the soprano, able to soar high but limited in its lower range. The cello (or violoncello, to give its full name) is like a bass-baritone, with the ability in its normal tuning to go down to the C two octaves below middle C, a couple of notes lower than most bass-baritones can sing. With the flexibility typical of string instruments, it can also play notes higher than a real (male) singer can cover—if it were a human voice it would include the tenor and some of the alto ranges, too. But surely the cello is best known and appreciated for the soulful, masculine timbre of its lower and middle ranges. Before Beethoven turned the cello sonata into an important, if relatively small, category of chamber music, there were the six astonishing suites for solo cello and three fine sonatas for viola da gamba and harpsichord, now commonly played by cello and piano, by Bach. The viola da gamba is an older instrument that is not exactly an ancestor of the cello, but which the later instrument mostly supplanted until it was revived by the early-music movement of the twentieth century. During this era, the other important composer for the instrument was Luigi Boccherini (1743–1805). A cellist himself, Boccherini had a feel for the instrument that was remarkable, and his compositions for it—mostly sonatas and concertos—make pleasing listening. Boccherini also composed string quartets and quintets that influenced Mozart.

Beethoven's five sonatas for cellos and piano, stronger in profile than Boccherini's, are better known and more popular. They straddle almost his entire career, from the early Op. 5 pair from 1796, to the high middle period mastery of the popular Op. 69 sonata

(1807–8), to the Op. 102 sonatas of 1815, which stylistically approach the late period, fitting awkwardly into the middle-period profile. And although the repertory for cello and piano is far smaller than that for violin and piano, it is distinguished, including good and great works by Franz Schubert, Robert Schumann, Frédéric Chopin, Johannes Brahms, Antonín Dvořák, Claude Debussy, Sergei Rachmaninoff, Sergei Prokofiev, Richard Strauss, Dmitri Shostakovich, Benjamin Britten, and others. Beethoven broke ground for this noble instrument.

The two sonatas of Op. 5 were apparently commissioned by the cello-playing King Friedrich Wilhelm II of Prussia, who also received dedications of string quartets by Mozart (the final three, K. 575, 589, and 590, known as the "King of Prussia" Quartets), and Haydn's Op. 50, six masterworks of 1787, known as the "Prussian" Quartets. Mozart's quartets feature prominent parts for the cello, but Haydn's do not. By all accounts, the king was an excellent cellist and a fine all-around musician. But Beethoven's two sonatas were written with a different player in mind—Jean-Louis Duport, principal cellist in the king's orchestra and one of the great instrumentalists of the age—so the cello parts of the sonatas, composed while Beethoven was in Berlin and working with Duport, are brilliant, difficult, and strictly for virtuosos. Both sonatas show Beethoven's early style in its full splendor, which is often surprising to listeners whose experience is limited to well-known pieces of the middle period. One of the great discoveries of a listener's life is making the acquaintance of these less familiar works, which show the energy, humor, craftsmanship, and passion of the young master. In addition to the two sonatas, Beethoven wrote while in contact with Duport two sets of variations for piano and cello: the first is on a noble theme from Handel's oratorio *Judas Maccabeus*; the second is based on the aria "Ein Mädchen oder Weibchen" from Mozart's *The Magic Flute*. A third set, from 1801, is also based on a duet ("Bei Männern, welche Liebe Fühlen") from the same opera. All are charming, second-tier works; but, as you might guess, even second-tier Beethoven is pretty fine.

Beethoven's Op. 5 sonatas are also notable for their two-movement structure, in which extended slow introductions open both works, leading directly into lively sonata-form allegros, and are followed by rondos.

There are, therefore, no slow movements—the weighty introductory passages more than satisfy the need for reflective, lyrically expressive parts that balance the works as a whole. As in the violin sonatas, Beethoven wrote equal parts for the two instruments, and it would be wrong to describe the pianist as an accompanist. And, as in the violin sonatas, the ensemble exchange between the two is as close as can be.

The slow introduction to the opening movement of the first sonata, in F major, occupies more than three of the movement's fourteen minutes of playing time. It commences quietly with a melodic figure shared by the instruments, after which the cello presents a long, lyrical phrase. Soon the piano takes on the main thematic burden. As the section moves toward its conclusion, Beethoven presents forcefully stated material in a sharper rhythmic pattern, followed by swirling figuration and a striking harmonic structure for the keyboard. The section has the feeling of a grand processional.

The main body of the movement is large in scale, with a profusion of thematic material. The opening theme, presented over a steady pulsing rhythm, is almost plain, but it's followed by a long, elaborate transitional passage leading to the second theme, presented initially by the cello and marked by a swaggering rhythm and an almost constant shifting between major and minor tonality. The closing group begins with swiftly moving chords for the piano, then another busy but grand transitional passage, and a final theme that's playful and kaleidoscopic. Beethoven moves first to A major, then to a mysterious D minor to begin the long development, also notable for its dark harmonies and a deep, long-held note for the cello that underpins the piano's shifts of key. The recapitulation displays an increased momentum and constant expansion of thematic material by a variety of means, including the addition of scales, trills, and repetitions of phrases. There's also a long cadenza before the final measures.

The rondo movements of both Op. 5 sonatas are enchanting. That of the F major work opens with a scampering dance for both instruments and is followed by a beauty of an episode in F minor marked by crisp pizzicati from the cello. The movement is also notable for having a sonata-like development of the themes. The second episode, in a distant key and pulse, strikes a faraway note; Beethoven brings it back for further consideration. The final episode dashes along furiously, but the composer brings things up short for an extended meditative passage before the final race to the end.

As fine as the F Major Sonata is, its companion work, the Sonata in G Minor, Op. 5 No. 2, is even better, a great example of Beethoven's youthful brilliance. The division of material between the instruments seems remarkably even here, so that you'll hear the piano accompanying the cello in the presentation of a theme, then the reverse; but in addition to the saturation of thematic material in both parts, the piano and cello also imitate each other, with the piano sometimes taking long melodic phrases while the cello plays busy, keyboard-like figuration.

The opening passage, nearly twice as long as its predecessor in Op. 5 No. 1, alternates a stark stalking rhythm with long, songful phrases for both instruments. Beethoven follows this with a fantasia-like passage featuring broad arpeggios (broken chords, reminiscent of the sound of a harp, *arpa* in Italian) for the keyboard alongside the cello's recitation of the stalking motif in a warmer incarnation, all bound to a gorgeously shifting harmonic structure. This gives way to a closing passage in which the cello seems to speak as the piano accompanies in an enriched version of the dotted stalking motif. The composer winds the whole introduction down to broken phrases for both instruments, interspersed with ever lengthening silences, in preparation for the main body of the movement. In this great introduction, all the weight of a slow movement is allied to a free structure and breadth of phrasing that give it genuine grandeur. The main part of the movement opens with the first subject, a sighing, waltzlike theme stated by the cello. Its gracefulness, following on the heels of the relentless four-beat rhythm of the opening section, makes a striking and powerful impression. The second theme group includes one resembling the familiar opening melody of Mozart's Symphony No. 40, also in G minor (short-short-long, short-short-long . . .) as the music takes on a more urgent momentum. Note the speed in the piano, from which racing triplets are rarely absent; also listen for the constant shift from major to minor in the second part of the swaying second subject group. The development includes the normal dissections and recombinations of thematic material but is unusually aggressive in tone, and a new theme emerges from the struggle. The recapitulation reverses the Mozartean theme, where it comes out long-short-short instead. Beethoven ends the movement in G major, preparing the way for the finale in that bright key.

While the rondo (CD Track 2) is fun to hear from start to finish, be aware that Beethoven experiments with form here, adding sonata-like development of some episodic material and varying the main rondo theme at each appearance. Also, the main theme is doubled by complementary phrases that reply differently every time, and that act as a tail to the main theme. Beethoven presents a generous series of ideas, the first of which is a cheerful theme stated by the piano. Its reply appears at 0:29. The lyrical first episode comes at 0:57, and its beautiful, sinuous second phrase at 1:30. The rondo reappears at 1:55, followed by a development-like tail at 2:20. The long second episode (2:53) features busy passagework for both instruments; its reply, which starts at 3:24, turns into another extended passage, also in the style of a development. Beethoven begins to tease the rondo theme back to life (4:26) with bits of its opening notes, finally allowing the tune to recur in full at 4:40. Then he does something unusual by bringing back the first episode (5:44) pretty much in its original shape, followed by the same tail as before (6:16). Classical-era rondos do not typically repeat episodes, but the form's playfulness seems to encourage Beethoven to try something different. In the final appearance of the main theme (6:40) Beethoven syncopates (puts accents on unexpected beats), then breaks it into showers of little notes for both instruments. The long, elaborate coda seems to reduce the main theme to a simpler formula, including the insertion of a completely new theme at 8:09. This is one of the master's most shapely and charming rondos, and a marvelous end to this first-period masterpiece.

Beethoven composed the Sonata in A Major for Cello and Piano, Op. 69, in 1808. It's the most popular of the five, and the longest, too. The master wrote "Amid tears and grief" in a copy of the score he gave to the work's dedicatee, but few can hear in its affect anything but tranquility. Its generous scale and richly melodious character have surely contributed to its popularity as well. The structure of Op. 69 is quite interesting: the first and last movements are in sonata form, and the second is a scherzo in a variant of the ABA pattern. A slow passage acts as a third, slow movement: though beautiful, it's only about ninety seconds long, serving as an introduction to the finale. Beethoven composed quite a few of these "shadow" slow movements in his career. These brief movements typically begin grandly, as a long slow movement might, then evaporate, often leading, as here, directly into the finale. Another important chamber work that follows this pattern is the String Quartet in C-sharp Minor, Op. 131, but there are more than a few in the Beethoven canon.

The cello quietly states the first theme, a memorable tune notable for its steady flow of calm quarter notes. The piano joins, in the same spirit, suddenly adding a short cadenza, which the cello soon echoes. After a pause, the second element, a tangy A minor variant of the opening theme, enters, marked by triplets in the piano. The second theme can be identified by rising scales for the cello over a sweet commentary by the piano, with the two instruments then reversing their roles as it's repeated. As in the "Kreutzer" Sonata for Violin and Piano (pp. 35–38) there's a third theme, to which the string part of this one bears some resemblance: above flowing triplets, the piano spins out a marchlike melody over proud pizzicati for the cello. A closing group, based on part of the first theme and marked by long trills for the piano, rounds out the exposition.

The development features a beautiful falling melody based on the opening quarter-note idea and a mock-stormy episode typical of such passages. Beethoven ends the section with a nearly still phrase of long-held notes. The recapitulation involves extensive expansion and elaboration of the thematic material. The trills of the closing group now lead into a long coda that is reflective and consistent in character with the tranquil affect of the movement.

As we've seen in three of the violin sonatas, a scherzo is usually in three sections, the first and third identical, or nearly so, and the middle of contrasting character. The Op. 69 scherzo is a little different, with the opening appearing three times and the second part twice (ABABA). With its A minor tonality and unsettling rhythmic patterns, this is the darkest movement in the sonata. The opening theme disturbs immediately, with its curt tune, abrupt shifts of dynamics (volume), and off-the-beat notes for the piano. Listen also to the very fast, lightly played octaves for the piano and the mournful commentary of the cello. Startling silences precede a shift in key toward A major, but this, too, is achieved over a galumphing rhythmic figure for the piano. A deep drone in the keyboard leads to the B section, which, despite its turn toward the major, maintains the nervous energy of the opening section. Beethoven works back swiftly to the opening passage, which is again repeated, as is the contrasting A major passage, and, once again, the opening strain; everything is boiled down to its essence in a short, spectral coda. The piano is the busier partner here, scrambling madly throughout, while the cello mostly adds syncopated single notes.

A grandly proportioned, operatic melody follows, played first by the piano, then by the cello. It sounds just like the kind of tune that opens many of the composer's great slow movements, but instead of any further development, after a little cadenza for the cello, the finale begins without pause. As noted, this movement is in sonata form, its opening theme in quarter notes stated by the cello over excited muttering by the piano. The lovely second subject consists of a questioning four-note phrase for the cello to which the piano makes a reply in murmuring eighth notes, ending with a stutter that's reminiscent of speech. The instruments race off excitedly in the closing theme. The development takes the opening theme into the minor key. The composer then quietly repeats the opening notes of the movement six times in a slippery chromatic phrase for the cello as the piano mutters repeated notes alongside. There's a racing passage with a contrapuntal inflection, then the chromatic passage with the instruments' roles reversed; this leads into the recapitulation and a big, beautiful coda. Here the first theme is stated ardently by the piano, with the cello singing just as passionately far below; then comes an expansive climax of the first theme and a glittering closing passage that seems to echo the final pages of the famous "Waldstein" Sonata for Piano, Op. 53, albeit less thunderously. But the closing episode stays faithful to the lyricism of this movement and the sonata as a whole.

Beethoven composed the two Sonatas for Cello and Piano, Op. 102, in 1815. As with the Op. 5 pair, the composer was in close contact with a master cellist, in this case the Viennese virtuoso Joseph Linke. The sonatas are products of the last phase of Beethoven's middle period, so utterly different in style from the early middle. Compositions like these, or the Piano Sonata in A Major, Op. 101, of 1816, have little in common stylistically with signature works of the middle period, like the A Major Cello Sonata, Op. 69, or the "Waldstein" and "Appassionata" Piano Sonatas. Where those sound spacious and lyrical, these seem more dense in texture and complex technically. You'll hear more counterpoint in the later works as Beethoven's reliance on the technique grows. Whereas a typical middle-period work will move in a clear trajectory from its opening toward a climactic ending, these may strike you as a bit more wayward, as though Beethoven is sometimes more occupied with surface details. His continuing tendency to make the finale a work's crucial movement is more obvious than ever, especially in the big fugal conclusion of Op. 102 No. 2, but the endings themselves are more relaxed, less violent, than in works from a decade earlier.

The Sonata No. 4 in C Major for Piano and Cello has an experimental five-movement structure. It parallels that of the four-movement Piano Sonata in E-flat Major, Op. 27 No. 1 (1802), in which the movements are played without pause and early material is recalled later in the work. The contemporaneous Piano Sonata Op. 101, with four movements, also presents a recollection of the opening passage later in the work. All these point toward the vast forms of the late string quartets, Opp. 130–132. The high-water mark of these tremendous works is Op. 131, with its seven movements played without pause and linked together thematically.

The opening section, introductory in function and noble in character, moves at a slowish tempo. It's lyrical but extremely complex, with countless expressive shifts of harmony and rhythm and an absolutely equal sharing of material by the two instruments. We can hear in this passage many of the characteristics of Beethoven's late style, including its density, freedom of form, and many trills, the sound of which obsessed the master's imagination in his later years. It's also interesting to note that nearly all the sonata's themes are derived from the first few bars, providing a unity and making the entire work a process of continuous development, another technique the composer used throughout his career. The sonata-form section that follows begins with a fiery theme in A minor that storms up then down in spiky detached notes, a clear call to battle that contrasts strongly with the opening and challenges the listener with its harshness. The second theme—more lyrical, even mournful, in character—is also richly harmonized. A defiant closing section, based on the first theme, rounds out the exposition. The development highlights the sharp rhythm of the first theme's falling second portion but is interrupted by a strange, still moment in which both instruments nearly stop on a sequence of quiet chords in a faraway harmony. Beethoven ends the movement on an expansion of the sharp rhythm of a three-note figure that closed the exposition.

The composer carefully indicated a one-bar rest before the beginning of the adagio, a somber interlude dominated by billowing figuration for the piano over which the cello sings a sorrowful descant. This unwinds in an open-ended lyrical passage marked by trills before moving directly into a repeat of the sonata's opening passage, with the material redistributed between the instruments. After the stormy sonata movement and the darkness of the adagio, our old friend's reappearance is welcome. An immensely long trill for the piano, in which the cello later joins, leads to the main theme of the finale, a rising four-note figure that seems to slip out inadvertently from the trill. Its playful introduction sets the character of the last movement, a comical sonata-form essay, flavored by counterpoint. Right away you'll notice the off accents and the bustling busy work Beethoven assigns the cello, as well as an abrupt phrase ending followed by pauses and then long notes in strange harmony for the cello. These play tag with the four-note opening phrase in a witty development, followed by a mock-serious fugato for both instruments. You'll want to pay attention to the beautiful shift in harmony and rhythm to triplets as the coda begins.

The final sonata, in D major, is cast in a more conventional three movements, with the outer ones in quick tempos and the central slow movement slow. The second and third movements are, however, connected. The first movement opens with a jubilant theme for the piano consisting of long, tolling notes and fast turns, followed by a sequence of falling turns. The cello responds with a rising figure that starts loud but drops in volume as it progresses, setting a pattern of behavior for themes that follow and making clear the tone of the work is lyrical rather than militant. The second part of the opening thematic group

moves at a more even pace, as does the second theme, a lovely, symmetrical tune. Beethoven builds the closing from the initial theme, with
the implications of the tolling notes played out more fully; but, again,
its apparent vehemence vanishes as the volume drops. The development
is based on the spinning figure, repeated by the cello in a rainbow of
harmonies, first against a chattering keyboard accompaniment, then
more quietly and eloquently. Beethoven continues the pattern of rising
excitement leading to fade-downs in the extended recapitulation and in
the coda, where quiet chords over a throbbing accompaniment dominate until the bustling final bars.

The second movement is the only full slow movement in the cello
sonatas. It's in a conventional ABA form, with the outer sections in
D minor and the more flowing middle part in D major. The opening
melody, solemn and almost austere, is stated by both instruments in
even notes; but soon a pulsing figure appears in the piano's left hand
part that accompanies a second melody based on vocal-sounding, almost
operatic turns. The key change to the tonic major lends a note of relief
to the gravity of this profound movement, as does a spinning figure
first stated by the piano, then explored repeatedly by both instruments.
When the opening section returns, the composer varies the material,
with the piano taking the theme while the cello decorates with a stark
falling figure. The operatic melody reappears with a more elaborate
piano accompaniment, which blends the falling figure just played by
the cello with an active pattern deep in the left hand. And Beethoven
changes harmony while nearly stopping all movement in a postlude of
the utmost solemnity; this also prepares the way for the last movement,
which follows without pause, introduced by two quick rising scales for
cello, then piano. These introduce the theme of the last movement,
Allegro fugato, and a sibling to the fugues in the last movements of the
Piano Sonatas Op. 101 and Op. 106 (the "Hammerklavier"), which
followed this work. The first part of the fugue, in three parts, introduced by the cello, is based on the rising scale and a tail in a curious
rhythm. Even with Beethoven's careful counterpoint, this grows into a
lumbering dance of considerable charm. After this fugue spins itself out
quietly, Beethoven introduces a second theme, presented by the cello
singing in its high register, which he develops into a chiming three-part

fugue, joyful in character. A sequence of long trills in the piano's left hand, culminating with an ecstatic twenty-bar trill on low D, sounds before the concluding bars, in which Beethoven plays rhythmically with his theme. Although the master plunges into arcane contrapuntal territory in this double fugue, its waltzlike pulse maintains the movement's consistent tone of delicacy and good humor.

The Trios

Beethoven's compositions for three instruments fall into two categories. First are the six trios for piano, violin, and cello in standard three- and four-movement sonata-based forms, called the piano trios. The composer also wrote two less ambitious but entertaining sets of variations for the ensemble. The second important but less familiar category in which Beethoven worked is for violin, viola, and cello, known as the string trios. All from his early period, these five works are serious and polished but are perhaps the least well-known of Beethoven's chamber compositions. They will serve us as an introduction to a new instrument—the viola—and to the sound of an all-string ensemble, as opposed to the piano and string mixes we've looked at so far. We'll consider the piano trios first.

As noted in chapter 1, Beethoven inherited the piano trio from Haydn and Mozart, whose contributions to the genre are significant. As mentioned earlier, the piano dominates Haydn's piano trios. Some listeners who have heard Beethoven's, Schubert's, or Dvořák's find Haydn's uneven distribution of material among the instruments hard to get used to. But musicians and audiences of greater experience know the astonishing richness of these piano trios. The pianist and musicologist Charles Rosen has been their advocate over the years, pointing out their absolute musical quality, no matter that the piano runs the show, as well as the dating of many to Haydn's high maturity in the 1790s.[1] Several that are sure to astonish the willing and attentive first-time listener are the A-flat Major, H. XV, No. 14; the G Major, H. XV, No. 25; the E Major, H. XV, No. 28; and the exquisite F-sharp Minor, H. XV, No. 26.

Five of Mozart's six piano trios also come from some of that master's high-tide years, 1786–88, but with the exception of the suave E Major Trio, K. 542, they are among the least performed of his chamber works, perhaps because of their relative restraint—the two piano quartets (K. 478 and 493), for example, their closest relations in the composer's oeuvre, are unquestionably bigger and bolder. Mozart raises the strings to equality with the keyboard in his trios. Even the earliest (K. 254, written in 1776) contains a charming pizzicato passage for the cello in its finale. The category went on to considerable enrichment by later composers, with Schubert's two piano trios ranking among his greatest chamber works; and Felix Mendelssohn, Schumann, Brahms, Bedřich Smetana, Dvořák, Pyotr Ilyich Tchaikovsky, Maurice Ravel, and Shostakovich all made important contributions to the genre.

Beethoven's six piano trios and the two sets of variations for the same ensemble are all large in scale and rich in musical technique and expression. The first three, published in 1795 as Beethoven's Op. 1, are four-movement works that display the young master's confidence and ambition. These were not Beethoven's first compositions—he had been writing music since he was eleven years old—but rather the first to which he granted the pedigree of an opus number. The third, in C minor, is a daring work that caused some friction between Beethoven and his teacher, Haydn, who advised the younger composer not to publish it. Haydn's exact words are not known, but Beethoven took them badly, concluding that Haydn was jealous of his talent and did not wish him well, which seems unlikely. The scale of the Piano Trio No. 1 in E-flat Major, Op. 1 No. 1, like its two companions in that opus number, is huge and often described as "symphonic."[2] This means that Beethoven expanded the genre beyond Mozart's and Haydn's dimensions, treating his material structurally as he would in a symphony. The earlier masters' trios are in three movements; Beethoven's Op. 1 are all in four. It's also worth noting that throughout this first trio the piano takes the leading role, without dominating to the same extent as in Haydn's piano trios.

The first movement opens with a brisk, rising figure, but almost immediately Beethoven throws in a harmonically unstable note that creates doubt in the ear about its key, displaying his already formidable sophistication. The second theme is a tranquil tune, moving in even notes. The exposition is rounded out by a dramatically phrased theme based on quietly rising triplets for the keyboard, followed by loud chords. The development section is long and complex, pitting various thematic fragments over triplets and uneasy rhythms in the piano's left hand. The recapitulation offers almost constant expansions and elaborations of the original material, and a long coda adds more recasting of the thematic material.

The second movement is a lyrical rondo based on an expansive melody stated first by the piano. The first episode features a nice dialogue for the strings, while in the second the composer digs into darker, deeper regions in a passionate minor key before turning unexpectedly to triumphant, thundering chords for the piano. The movement ends with a delicate coda. A really fine scherzo is marked initially by a swaying theme, immediately after which the composer works in all kinds of rhythmic and harmonic surprises. The theme of the trio soars lyrically in contrast with the drive of the movement's outer sections. Based on a fiddly, lighter-than-air theme stated by the piano, the sonata-form finale races along in a comical vein. The second theme is a busy, cheerful tune with a Hungarian flavor and a rhythmically condensed tail. The development begins in a mock-*furioso* mood, but the more thoughtful passage that follows cools things down. In the very long recapitulation, the composer takes an extended if not exactly leisurely second look at the themes, making unexpected Haydnesque silences and one hilarious outburst part of his compositional vocabulary. One of the most remarkable openings to any composer's career, this astonishing work leaves little doubt as to its creator's potential.

Beethoven opens the G Major Trio, Op. 1 No. 2, with a ceremonious slow introduction: the piano indulges in a passionate and virtuosic display against the more lyrical string parts, which from the start take a greater role than they did in the first trio. The opening subject of the main part of the movement is a jolly theme in a dancelike rhythm based on a repeated note followed by a turn. Pay attention when you listen to how carefully Beethoven balances the three instruments' parts and to his use of dynamics—the volume at which the music is played: he moves from loud to soft in a instant, requiring tight coordination on the part of the performers. The second subject, in a more high-strung metrical pattern, is first stated by the violin, with a light piano accompaniment, and the comical closing theme takes its cue from its jumpy predecessor. The mood of the development is more serious because Beethoven moves into a minor key and treats the material contrapuntally, always a mark of erudition in the classical era. In parts of this relatively long section, the cello unmistakably takes the lead. As is normal for Beethoven, the recapitulation sounds like a second development; this one also contains a false ending on thunderous chords before continuing quietly, in a mock-innocent manner.

There's much to admire in the second movement, marked *largo con espressione* (broadly and expressive), including Beethoven's bold choice of E major for its key—unusual in the classical era for a composition in G major—and its elevated tone. Its form is a double variation, based on two long themes. The piano states the first, a noble melody in swaying rhythm and richly harmonized, which the strings soon join. The second, also introduced by the keyboard with commentary first by the violin, then the cello, is a more passionate tune of repeated notes in a stabbing rhythm. What follows are alternating variations on the two melodies. Here again the composer shows his ambition by using richly affective material in a complex form and dense harmonic scheme, all of which he handles with unerring assurance. The scherzo more or less follows the pattern of its predecessor in the E-flat major trio, with perhaps a bit less warmth. It starts with a lilting tune into which the composer introduces rhythmic irregularities. The trio (the middle section) is a more pungent dance, marked by rustic moments, particularly for the cello and a long trill for the piano. And the finale, based on a manic and wiggly figure for the violin, is a riotous essay in sonata form very much in the spirit of Haydn, with abrupt silences and changes of tempo and key. But the melting third theme has the poise to calm the otherwise madcap proceedings. The development section seems wild and angry, but as is often the case, the rage is revealed as mere theatrics, vanishing as soon as the next, more cheerful idea happens along. Beethoven ends the movement on the opening wiggle, banged out by the three instruments with great energy.

The third trio, in C minor—the one that gave Haydn pause—was Beethoven's favorite of the three and is the finest in Op. 1, a work of power and magnificence, closer perhaps to a Mozartean model. Beethoven would of course go on to compose a great deal in C minor; but the use of C minor, and all minor ("sad") keys, was for Mozart much more uncommon. (Beethoven made their use almost normal.) Mozart's compositions in C minor all share rich sound and a feeling of violent drama, while maintaining his normal grace, that also applies to Beethoven's Op. 1 No. 3, particularly its first movement. The opening themes of Mozart's Piano Concerto No. 24, K. 491, and of the Beethoven trio are similar in melodic and metrical profile, both ominous but quickly arching gracefully off in a dancelike triple meter.

That opening theme, stated in unison by the three instruments, is a rocking melody, animated by a couple of lyrical turns, then a convulsive slowdown that anticipates the first movement of the "Kreutzer" Sonata. It's then restated, chiefly by the piano in a slightly different but more urgent guise. The second theme, presented by the piano and violin in a more soothing E-flat major, is clearly derived from the opening idea. The violin and cello state the closing theme, marked by a sudden drop in volume and a more lyrical character than its companions, over a flowing keyboard accompaniment. Note, when you listen, the stabbing accents with which Beethoven liberally punctuates so much of the exposition. Similar explosions and rhythmic disturbances mark the development, which opens with a discussion, initiated by the piano, of the first theme. The long, flowing lines all three instruments play again suggest Mozart more than Haydn as the model here, but the sense that the music is straining at its formal and expressive limits is authentically Beethoven's.

A set of five variations on a lyrical two-part theme assumes the position of second movement, offering relief from and contrast with the rigors of the opening. The piano elaborates the theme in the first variation while the strings add simple decoration; in the second variation, violin and cello render the theme in flowing sixteenth notes while the piano keeps to the background. Beethoven creates a bright sound for the contrapuntal third variation by having the strings play pizzicato against the piano's glittering runs. The fourth variation presents the theme in compressed shape in the tonic minor key (E-flat minor), ending in a drooping phrase that falls in volume as well as pitch. The cello plays the melody in the amiable fifth variation, with piano and violin decorating quite elaborately. Rounding the movement out, Beethoven adds a coda, where he blends the compression of the fourth variation with the decorative figuration of the fifth.

Although the C Minor Trio is the most forward-looking member of the Op. 1 set, Beethoven makes its third movement an apparently old-fashioned menuetto, rather than a more modern scherzo. But as you listen to the menuetto, you'll perceive that it's a rather grim and abstract example, following in the affect of the opening movement, with no sense of courtliness and little feeling of the dance except in its middle section, which sounds a bit like a country round. Beethoven marks the tempo at the start of the ferocious finale *prestissimo*—very quick. It begins with a savage rising gesture, thumped out by the three instruments together. Here the affect is unambiguously furious, with no hint of pretending. A pleading melody sung first by the violin in even notes follows, and the second theme feels a bit more clement with its shift to E-flat major in even half notes that seem to slow the pace. But in fact Beethoven never slackens his tempo. The development is notable for an urgent contrapuntal treatment of the second theme. Beethoven's ending is stunning: he shifts to C major and drops the volume, ending this violent, minor-key-driven structure softly in a melodramatic, harmonically cloudy phrase.

Fourteen years separate the Op. 1 trios from their successors, the Op. 70 pair of 1808; other compositions of 1808 include the Fifth and Sixth Symphonies and the A Major Sonata for Piano and Cello, Op. 69. The two trios form a balanced pair, with the first, a powerful and experimental three-movement work in D major, contrasting with the more good-humored E-flat major, in the standard (for Beethoven) four movements. One critic views the Op. 70 trios and the preceding cello sonata as a trilogy, because "they develop new ways of blending and opposing string and keyboard roles that radically revise earlier patterns."[3] Lockwood cites the greater roles Beethoven assigns the strings as well as the increased difficulty of all the parts in these formidable compositions, which you will notice immediately, particularly when you listen to the D Major Trio.

Nicknamed the "Ghost," the Trio in D Major, Op. 70 No. 1, is a daring conception. The work's unusual structure and nickname derive from the weight and significance the composer gives to the spooky central slow movement. Both outer movements are in quick tempos, with the first acting as a prelude and the third relieving—somewhat— the tensions generated by the second. In case you haven't grasped the concept of ensemble, the opening of the D Major Trio—a headlong scramble of notes, played in unison by all three instruments—will tell you what the term means. Only three virtuosos, who must still work hard to coordinate their attack, can play the furious opening phrase, in which key and rhythm are at first impossible to make out. The theme is based on a combination of the D major chord and scale, but as he often does, Beethoven throws in a couple of notes that make the harmony ambiguous. It's reminiscent of the first movement of the G Major Sonata for Piano and Violin (CD Track 1, discussed on pp. 34–35) and looks ahead to first theme of the D Major Cello Sonata, Op. 102 No. 2 (pp. 49–51), but is wilder than either. The remainder of the opening thematic group consists of a sequence of less spiky melodic phrases that melt gradually toward the second theme, which consists of rocking chords in the piano followed by scales against a strong lilting rhythm for violin and cello. The closing theme is a breathtakingly scored proto-romantic beauty, and a relief to the ear in its clear allegiance to one key. The development starts with a contrapuntal feeling, but Beethoven soon abandons this approach for a modulatory sequence through a thicket of keys before returning to the opening group. As always, the composer expands and embellishes his material in the recapitulation. The restatement of the closing theme sounds even more glorious than it did the first time around, and the movement ends with a coda that starts lyrically, with the second tune of the first thematic group, but ends with the avalanche of notes that began this exercise in momentum.

The form of the second movement is a theme with four variations, but it's primarily a study in the use of spectral tone color to express the gloomiest affect. The four variations are, in fact, all quite similar in sound and tempo, so that the effect is one of anxious and oppressive unity rather than the variety of thematic treatments we heard in other variation sets, such as the second movement of the C Minor Trio,

Op. 1 No. 1, or the second movement of the "Kreutzer" Sonata. Strings and keyboard share the statement, consisting of a series of broken phrases, including turns for the piano and longer, wailing notes for the strings woven into a long, despairing melody. The tempo, *largo assai ed espressivo*, or "very broad and expressive," is one of Beethoven's slowest, adding to the gravity of the music. Soon the three instruments break into a loud, melodramatic harmony, common to deliberately spooky music in the nineteenth century, as the piano begins a series of trembling accompaniments that holds almost without pause until the last few bars. These are not one figure, but a variety of trills and *tremolandi*— handfuls of trembling notes—in weird harmonies, sometimes deep in the bass and others higher up, for bars on end; these are tiring to play and oppressive in effect. The strings play variants of the long theme, some quite violent, and some above, others below the almost continual shuddering of the keyboard; from time to time the piano shares thematic responsibility, but mostly it accompanies. You'll observe when you listen that the obsessive repetitions of the melodic phrases—the turns, for example—become genuinely disturbing as the instruments grind them out, harder and harder, over the course of the movement. The trembling also ceases for a bleak little coda.

The finale, the most conventional movement in the "Ghost" Trio, is based on an even-tempered theme that moves mostly in quick but steady quarter notes, stated first by the piano, which is soon joined suavely by the violin and cello. But the piano has an odd, improvisatory solo near the end of the exposition that displays Beethoven's eccentricity as well as his absolute freedom in the handling of material. Some pizzicati please the ear, and a tranquil dialogue for cello and piano in the development section helps soothe frayed nerves. Another chiming passage for plucked strings and the piano, imitating the strings' sound, kicks off the upbeat closing measures.

The character of the E-flat Major Trio, Op. 70 No. 2, is commonly described in terms of its difference from that of its demonic D major companion. The moods of the two trios are indeed far apart. But the second trio of the opus is, in its less obvious way, just as unconventional, displaying countless peculiarities of structure and detail. Like several other important works in the Beethoven canon (the Piano Sonata No.

18, Op. 31 No. 3; and the Seventh Symphony), the trio has no real slow movement. Instead, its two central movements, both moderate in tempo and very close in speed, look ahead to Beethoven's late style and beyond. The key structure of the four movements is also unusual. Furthermore, the first movement has a slow introduction that recurs later, and the big finale also presents listeners with more than a few difficulties in its themes and their developments.

The first movement begins with a long, gentle introductory passage that casts a spell over the entire movement. Beethoven gives it the rare and significant tempo marking *poco sostenuto*, meaning "a little sustained"; the term *sostenuto* requires that the notes "be sustained to their full value in a smooth flow."[4] Beethoven was to use this marking once more for the majestic opening passage of the Symphony No. 7 (1811–12). This introduction shares with its successor a deep lyricism, though not its enormous scale. The cello, joined first by the violin, then by the keyboard, sets the searching tone for the passage, whose key seems unclear at the start, with a sequence of trills and *appogiature*—sliding resolutions of a dissonance—adding to both the sense of uncertainty and the richness of sound. Finally, having suggested the home key of E-flat major without actually settling on it, Beethoven carefully moves into its dominant key of B-flat major, which in the classical harmonic vocabulary leads the listener's ear to expect that E-flat major will follow. This it does, with a mellow tune for all three instruments. The music also shifts from the steady, four-beat pulse of the introduction to a lilting 6/8 meter, ripe with pastoral associations, in a quicker though still not too rapid tempo. The first thematic group continues with an earthier version of the theme, sung out lustily by the violin and piano with the cello sawing away below, and a new version of the opening melody of the introduction, covered in even notes by the piano and cello. The tempo sounds identical to that of the introduction, but in fact Beethoven has adapted it metrically to its new setting. The second theme follows, more fluid and built on flowing passagework for the violin and piano; then comes a long closing theme marked by trills and busy scales for the piano. The brief development includes a passage for the keyboard in which the hands play far apart, very high and very low on the keyboard—a hallmark of Beethoven's piano style. There's also an episode of fantastically rich harmony and lots of ecstatic trills. Beethoven sneaks the beginning of the recapitulation in so that it's not obvious, adding to the overall sense of lyrical flow. The recapitulation elaborates all the thematic material considerably, as does the long coda, in which the composer reprises the opening *poco sostenuto* phrases before the closing bars, bringing the music satisfyingly full circle. It's also a good example of the master's rear-end loading, whereby in the course of his career he throws ever greater emphasis on the ends of movements.

The second and third movements stand together as two of Beethoven's boldest inspirations. Instead of a slow movement and a minuet or scherzo, we get two movements in similar, moderate tempos but of sharply different characters; both are also in unusual keys (C major and A-flat major, respectively) for a classical-era sonata-form composition in E-flat major. The second movement is clearly based on dance; the third is harder to pin down, displaying elements of song and dance. Most significantly, the music Beethoven composed for his unusual structures is startling.

On paper, the second movement consists of nothing more than two variations on the two dances stated at the outset to which a coda is added; but this description does little to capture the complexity and humor of this movement. The first dance, genial in character, is marked by a tickling rhythmic figure that's hard to forget, and the tune itself is sweet (even a bit sugary), relaxed, and in C major. The second dance, a far more rustic stamping affair, is in C minor, to which the composer shifts freely in mid-measure. It's so heavy-footed that the contrast with its airborne companion is really funny. With each alternating variation Beethoven takes the dichotomy further, contrasting the elegance of the first dance with the peasant-like clomping of the second. Triplets, for example, add to the suavity of the first in its first variation, while huge, biting chords from the strings, especially the cello, make quite an earful of the second variation of the rustic dance. But the long *diminuendo*—fade-down—that connects the second variation with the coda goes wittily against its character as we have known it. When you listen to it, you'll notice the cello's important, often hilarious contributions to the obsessive detail of the writing, as well as Beethoven's dynamic scheme, which is crucial to the music's effect. Its influence can be felt in Beethoven's own late work, notably the third movement of the Op. 130 string quartet (CD Track 8), and on later composers, including Schumann and Mahler, both of whom loved to rub the musically rough against the smooth.

The third movement is only slightly less astonishing than the second. It's in three parts, the opening being a long, songlike theme over a rocking accompaniment by the keyboard—proto-Mendelssohnian, in case you're familiar with that composer's placid melodic style. The middle section, however, features a hard-to-grasp (though very beautiful) theme consisting of a rustic but solemn call-and-response, with the call from the strings and the reply by the piano; it feels remote and hard to connect with the opening idea. An even weirder passage follows, a wheezily delicate chromatic chord sequence, resembling a Chopin mazurka in which the bagpipe is imitated, or a take-off on a peasant dance by Mahler. Into this the composer works some triplets for the piano, which begin to loosen things up. The melodious opening section is repeated, but the bagpipe sound and triplets come back once more before the opening tune ends the movement.

The finale, a large-scale essay in sonata form, can be a tough nut the first few times you listen, for Beethoven subjects his vigorous thematic material to vigorous treatment. Following an opening flourish, the instruments present the first theme, a tune with a hop at its end, which blends into a sequence where Beethoven changes everything that can change: the steady rhythm of the opening slips into melting triplets, the harmony jumps abruptly to remote keys, and the volume veers wildly from loud to soft and back again; only the tempo stays the same. The second theme, a stiff-gaited tune, points ahead to some of Beethoven's late-period works, notably the Great Fugue, Op. 133, of 1825–26. The closing idea moves between a delicate, hopping rhythm and furious sixteenth notes for the piano against stark rhythmic figures that echo the second subject in the strings. The short development includes a battle between the instruments that may be playful or earnest—it's hard to tell. And the massive recapitulation and coda restate and redevelop the opening material at great length and power. Yet among the instrumental wars lurk a few welcome quiet passages, such as the soft and lyrical opening of the coda, which concludes in massive, shuddering chords for all three instruments.

The two central movements of Op. 70 No. 2 helped to change the complexion of music, allowing composers to sequence sections of their multimovement works freely as the overall character and flow of the work itself demanded. Brahms's Third Symphony has two middle movements in relaxed, moderate tempos; and if you've heard Mahler's Second and Third Symphonies, you'll recall that the second and third movements of both are similarly structured, in moderate tempos and based on song and dance themes that contrast with each other slightly, but much more with the huge and violent opening movements they follow. Brahms and Mahler knew their Beethoven and unquestionably used the earlier master's groundbreaking procedure as precedent.

Sixth and last of the full-scale piano trios is the Op. 97 in B-flat Major, nicknamed the "Archduke," after Archduke Rudolph, Beethoven's most important patron and the dedicatee of this and many others of the composer's major compositions. Written in 1811, the "Archduke" Trio is the best-known and most frequently recorded of the six. It's a spacious middle-period work in the master's lyrically grand manner, rather like that of the A Major Cello Sonata, Op. 69 (pp. 45–47), both works being dominated by long, calm melodic patterns.

The "Archduke" Trio's most interesting structural feature is the placement of the magnificent scherzo as the second movement, then the slow movement (CD Track 3) as the third. This Beethoven does only rarely, and only where the overall balance of the composition demands it. Another important example of his placing the scherzo second is in the "Hammerklavier" Sonata for Piano, Op. 106, where the finale follows the slow movement, radically different though they are emotionally and musically. Yet another case is the Symphony No. 9, where the scherzo's energy helps to dispel the terrors of the first movement, leaving the third-movement adagio as a bridge to the finale. Each instance obeys its own aesthetic and logic. Here Beethoven connects the lofty third movement, the magical effect of which might be trivialized by a scherzo, and the showy but genial fourth. The "Archduke" is not only grand in scale but of the highest caliber, too, making its composition in a single month—March 1811[5]—all the more stupefying for mortals to consider.

The first movement opens directly with the first subject, stated by the piano—noble and serene, in an easy striding rhythm, with one marchlike bump (long-short-*long*) to break the notes' otherwise steady flow. The second portion of the first subject group features triplets for the piano over long-held turns and chords in remote harmonies for the strings, widening the scope of the movement's thematic inventory. The second group starts with a tune in repeated eighth notes, not unlike the second subject of the finale of the Op. 69 cello sonata; scales for the piano over a rich melody for the cello form the closing theme of the exposition. Beethoven pits the triplets and even quarter notes of the opening group against each other in the fantasia-like development, in which the harmony hovers rather than roams widely, as is more common in these passages. Then the master comes up with a particularly wonderful idea: the strings take up the opening phrase in pizzicato against bright trills for the piano in a long, aurally pleasing march, ultimately leading to a restatement of the opening and a very expansive recapitulation. The cello joins the piano in a leading role, with flourishes that beautify the themes as they pass once more in procession. An extended, mysterious, and ultimately ecstatic coda ends the movement.

The scherzo is a great example of Beethoven's wit, lyricism, and utter strangeness, in starkest juxtaposition. The movement opens with a humorous, rhythmically tightened parody of the first movement's main idea in 3/4 time, stated first by the cello, then the violin, and finally the piano. Soon the humor turns to joy as the keyboard sings it in the blissful high register, with the violin and cello adding plucked commentary. Next, the strings take the melody, with the piano accompanying. The middle section opens with a weird, arrhythmic, almost atonal theme in the cello which the piano and violin soon join. Beethoven interrupts this twice, improbably, with a surging waltz. He reduces the theme to its barest rhythmic profile, much like in the scherzo of the F Major String Quartet, Op. 59 No. 1, which we'll examine in chapter 10. A coda reasserts the weird theme of the trio before ending the movement on its primary thematic idea.

One of Beethoven's most inspired slow movements, the "Archduke" Trio's third (CD Track 3) consists of a theme and five variations. It's a majestic example of the master's most elevated style, beginning with an idea of beauty and joyful deep feeling, then with each variation deepening its expressivity and bliss. The two-part theme itself is given by the piano, which the strings then join in repeat, making its initial statement a spacious twenty-four bars. The effect is more hymnlike than arialike, and the tempo not particularly slow. The first variation (1:52) gives a boiled-down version of the theme to the strings, with the cello entering first, while the piano renders the melody in fervent triplets. In the second variation (3:27), the strings break the theme into mincing sixteenth notes accompanied by the keyboard, often in rapid, detached figuration. Throbbing sixteenth-note triplets and the richest harmony dominate the third variation (4:43), which breaks into open ecstasy. The tempo slows a bit for the glorious fourth variation (6:07), which in its songful rapture anticipates the Ninth Symphony's slow movement and also the variations in the final piano sonatas, all of which can claim this movement as a clear antecedent. As you listen, note how the three instruments share the melodic material, while the swiftly flowing piano accompaniment provides ceaseless trembling accompaniments that trace and enhance melody and harmony—another striking characteristic that blossoms even more luxuriantly in Beethoven's late-period variations. The fifth variation (8:33) is a profound meditation on what has passed before. Throbbing keyboard triplets at 9:45 intensify the emotion as the music seems to float toward its conclusion. The last chord is expectant rather than conclusive, and the finale follows without pause.

Beethoven changes mood with surprising ease from the sublimities of the slow movement to a jovial, very Viennese rondo on a dancelike theme with a bit of a swagger, stated by the piano. And the piano clearly dominates this movement, keeping busy with a glittering and virtuosic role while the strings remain subordinate. The two episodes share a broader, more harmonically ambiguous character, and Beethoven ends the movement with a long, up-tempo, and difficult coda into which he introduces material from the main theme and the episodes. The final bars, marked *più presto* (faster), transform the theme into a racing tarantella that also had a major effect on Schubert, who used the same rhythm in more than one finale.

These are the six important sonata-form piano trios, but you'll find that complete recorded sets include a few other works. The three-movement Trio in B-flat Major, Op. 11, a polished work from 1798 originally conceived for piano, cello, and clarinet, is better heard in its first incarnation—the violin which Beethoven authorized in place of the clarinet can't rival the wind instrument's sweetness and charm. Its first movement offers a delicate interplay between the three instruments, with contrasting themes in a briskly paced sonata form. The second movement is an adagio in which the liquid tone of the clarinet sings passionately; the finale is a charming set of eight variations on a simple theme by Joseph Weigl, a contemporary of Beethoven's known for his operettas. Listen for the switch to a lilting 6/8 rhythm and the unusual distribution of material in the eighth variation and coda. Another gem in recorded complete trio sets is likely the solitary and sweet Allegretto in B-flat Major of 1812, identified by the number WoO 39 (the initials stand for *Werke ohne Opuszahl*, German for "works without opus number"). This pulsing, lyrical movement in dance rhythm, mature in style, is as lovely as it can be. It's also remarkably anticipatory of Schubert at his melodious best.

Beethoven also composed two important sets of variations for piano trio. The first, apparently from 1791, is based on a theme of comical simplicity by the German composer Karl Ditters von Dittersdorf. Beethoven runs with the ball, writing fourteen amusing variations in a variety of styles, most clever in variation 6, the hammering of which looks far ahead to the opening of the "Ghost" Trio, and impressively serious in variations 7 and 13, where he milks the inane little tune for sorrows beyond what you might have imagined it held. Variations 9 through 12 make up a dashing Mozartean overture, and the final numbered variation actually contains three new incarnations. This sophisticated effort by the twenty-year-old Beethoven carries an opus numbering of 44, suggesting it's from his middle period. It was not published until 1804, however, when the misleading sequencing was given.

The other set of variations for piano trio, ten on "Ich bin der Schnieder Kakadu," Op. 121a, has a similar history. The original work

dates from 1803. It was revised in 1816 when Beethoven tried unsuc-
cessfully to sell it, and may have been tweaked again in 1824, when it
was finally published. Also like Op. 44, the "Kakadu" Variations are
comical in spirit. The theme, by Wenzel Müller, is from a light opera,
similar in many ways—except for its quality—to "Der Vogelfänger
bin ich, ja" from Mozart's *The Magic Flute*. Beethoven makes the little
tune sound good, however, subjecting to it sophisticated treatments:
light counterpoint in variations 5, 7, and 10; throbbing syncopation
in variation 8; and some really funny barnyard squeals for the strings
set against a racing piano part in variation 6. Variation 9 is a moving
imitation of a Mozartean aria in the relative minor key. But the most
striking section of the work is the introduction, a long, doom-laden
passage where the theme is prefigured in what we hear in retrospect
as an incongruous wail before emerging in its own absurd simplicity as
the subject. Rachmaninoff, in the *Rhapsody on a Theme by Paganini*, and
Ernč Dohnányi in the *Variations on a Nursery Song*, successfully adapted
Beethoven's witty insertion of variations before the official statements
of their themes. And the final variation is expansive, actually containing
two variants and a sizable coda, balancing the long introduction and
providing the "Kakadu" Variations with a pleasing symmetry. Both Op.
44 and Op. 121a show Beethoven's natural inclination for the variation
form while also anticipating his greatest set: the *Diabelli Variations*,
Op. 120, for piano, where the master exalts another worthless theme
in thirty-three mind-blowing incarnations.

The String Trios

Beethoven wrote five important compositions for the ensemble consisting of violin, viola, and cello. All date from the early and mid-1790s—
the last was completed in 1798—with low opus numbers (Opp. 3, 8,
and 9) to match. There are fewer recordings of the string trios than of
any of Beethoven's major chamber works, reflecting their relative lack
of popularity; though serious and well-made, they have not really caught
the ear or imagination of the musical community or the listening public.
This may be due to their lean scoring: the heft of one additional violin in

the sound of a string quartet is obvious even to inexperienced listeners. After these five works, Beethoven never took up the ensemble again, focusing instead on the string quartet. He expressed pride in them, however, calling the three Op. 9 trios "the best of his works" when they were published. Certainly the C Minor Trio, Op. 9 No. 3, will engage any attentive listener, and individual movements in the other string trios (the last movement of the G Major, Op. 9 No. 1, for instance) are also fine. One strategy in approaching the string trios might be to get to know Op. 9 No. 3 first; another would be to tackle them as a group once you've gained some familiarity with the early string quartets.

New to the trio mix is the viola, a throaty instrument that looks like a bigger version of a violin and covers a range that combines that of tenor and alto singers, with the flexibility shared by all stringed instruments to hit notes that are considerably higher. Beethoven was trained to play the viola and performed on it in his youth with the Bonn court orchestra; Mozart liked to play it too. Its role is usually subordinate, holding the middle voice of the three, lacking the high singing power of the violin and the cello's depth of tone, acting as a kind of timbral glue that binds the higher and lower strings together. And of course it's one of the four instruments in a string quartet, the others being the two violins and the cello.

The Op. 9 trios are four-movement works in tight sonata form. Opus 8 is a serenade with five movements, lighter in tone than the other four works. And Op. 3, the earliest of these compositions, is a divertimento, another name for a work of several movements, supposedly a lighter musical "diversion." Haydn composed them, as did Mozart. Few would describe Mozart's divertimenti as light, least of all his profound and flawless Divertimento for String Trio, K. 563, of 1788. This masterwork must have influenced Beethoven in his thinking about the string trio, and it casts a long shadow—"incomparably the largest and grandest work in existence for string trio"[6]—over the genre. Beethoven's Op. 3 divertimento for string trio shares several features with Mozart's, including the key (E-flat major) and the number of movements (six), but does not challenge the supremacy of the older master's work in this admittedly small category.

Beethoven's divertimento for string trio opens promisingly with an exciting gesture of a pulsing, syncopated chord followed by a march figure, reminiscent of some of the openings of Mozart's piano concertos and opera overtures. Beethoven follows this with a more suave melody. The second theme, in a sprightly rhythm, anticipates the opening subject of Beethoven's first string quartet. The closing theme, a cool, chordal figure summoning faraway harmonies, is the most interesting of all. The second movement, a more curious affair in a moderate tempo (andante), moves in short notes and, with its frequent shifts of key from major to minor and the rumbling of the cello trilling in its deepest register, is not a moment of calm. The menuetto that follows opens with a pause-laden theme in a skeletal rhythm that makes the listener wonder what's coming next; the tune of the trio is contrastingly long-limbed, gorgeous, and underpinned by pleasing pizzicati for the cello. An operatic melody, given mostly to the violin, is the chief pleasure in the slow rondo that is the fourth movement. The most striking moment comes just before the final recurrence of the rondo theme, where Beethoven gives the three instruments a snarling chordal sequence that turns prayerful at the end. Another, more standard menuetto than the third movement follows; listen for the charming bagpipe imitation that the composer uses for the trio. The finale is another rondo, this one based on a quirky Haydnesque theme that Beethoven passes cleverly among the instruments. The composer adds a striking meditation in slow tempo just before the brisk closing.

The Serenade in D Major, Op. 8, of 1796–97, is the most playful of the works for string trio. It opens and closes with a mockingly pompous march that from the second measure features big three- and four-string chords that generate such a surprising volume level and are this work's signature sound. In general, the serenade is more reliant on instrumental effects and less on abstract forms and ideas than are its companion works. The three-part adagio that is the second movement is a convincing take-off on the Italian operatic style, with the violin taking the part of the singer in the warm outer sections; the middle part expresses a more pained affect. The sound of huge chords kicks off the menuetto, for which the composer also provides a delicate and witty coda for plucked instruments. The imaginative fourth movement alternates two sections, a mournful song for violin and viola over a steadily moving accompaniment by the cello and a scurrying scherzo in which the cello scratches out big but quick chords, creating a stark contrast with the opening section. The linked adagio and scherzo repeat once more, then Beethoven ends the movement with the mournful opening passage. Apparently the adagio tells the story of a lover pouring his heart out to the object of his affection, who rejects him firmly in the scherzo passages.[7] A colorful Allegretto alla Polacca follows, in the prancing rhythm that characterizes this Polish dance, later brought to its highest peak by Chopin in his grand polonaises for piano. Again, though, huge chords for all three instruments saturate the texture of the score. The final section of this spacious work is a set of six variations on an easygoing two-part theme. The viola gets a rare chance to show off a bit in the second variation, and the stabbing syncopations of the third, in D minor, offer greater tension. Beethoven cleverly prepares the way at the end of the sixth variation for the return of the opening march, which rounds the work out.

Beethoven composed the three trios for strings published as his Op. 9 in 1797–98. Like the Op. 1 Piano Trios, the first two are in major keys, and the third is in the composer's favorite key of C minor. The first two trios are polite and expansive, the third ferocious and highly compressed. As usual, working in C minor seems to have set Beethoven's imagination on fire, sparking the best piece in the set; an important critic compares the String Quartet Op. 18 No. 4, also in C minor, unfavorably to the Op. 9 No. 3 trio.[8] It also seems to be that rare commodity, a sleeper in Beethoven's familiar oeuvre.

The G Major Trio, Op. 9 No. 1, begins with a slow introduction that's gracious and imposing at the same time. This leads directly into a smooth first theme which contrasts sharply with the second subject, a temporizing march in short chords. The closing group features a scampering figure that resembles the opening subject of the first string quartet of Op. 18. The development features a contrapuntal discussion; the recapitulation is notable for some interesting harmonic shading of the opening theme; and the coda features a passage in tremolando for the viola. The second movement is a leisurely Italianate aria rendered for three strings, remarkable, like its opposite number in the piano trios, for being in E major, an unusual key for a classical-era composition in G major; even early in his career Beethoven's harmonic imagination roams freely. The middle section begins with spinning figuration for the cello, which underlies panting chords for the violin and viola, and the big opening tune returns to end the movement. The scherzo opens with a perky melody that soon rides a chugging figure in the lower strings. The middle section of this ABA movement is set in lowish notes running in a steady rhythm that comically runs out of gas just before the return of the opening part.

The brilliant finale, surely the most interesting movement, is a shimmering sonata-form scramble that may remind you of the overtures to Mozart's comic operas. The second subject soars, then falls somewhat oddly over a staccato accompaniment. Then comes a more standard, flowing subject, and the third theme, in falling eighth notes for all the players, generates an impressive density of sound. Beethoven recasts the second theme in the development by inverting it and placing it in a setting of mysterious-sounding harmonies. And he winds the work up with a page of furious brilliance in which the three instruments remind you of a whole orchestra; it clearly foreshadows Beethoven's *Leonore* Overture No. 3, with its avalanche for racing strings.

The second trio, in D major, seems the best mannered and least arresting of the set, but it is still a fine work. The opening movement's first theme enters quietly in suave quarter notes, followed by more animated squeals for the violin; the second group opens with another smooth tune for violin and viola, with the cello pulsing below. The third theme, initiated by the viola, has more rhythmic kick. Beethoven passes the squealing figure from violin to viola and back again in the development and later in the passage down to the cello, which echoes it forcefully. The second movement is one of Beethoven's trademark slow movements that isn't really slow. It's a sad rondo that opens in curious two-note phrases suggesting strong emotion before moving on to more standard long lines. The broken phrases come back again and again, more strikingly each time.

The best part of the menuetto is the trio, where the composer plays delicately with detached notes for the three instruments in a variety of funny and charming melodic, harmonic, and instrumental combinations. The closing rondo features a breakout passage for the cello right at the start, marked "solo," where the instrument sings the opening tune in its tenor register. The second episode roams far afield harmonically, and the droning closing passage is echoed in the master's later stylistic developments.

As noted, the C Minor trio is the best of the set, a taut and dramatic work in which Beethoven's passion and structural inventiveness seem fully engaged, resulting in a satisfying early-period masterwork that deserves to be better known. The trio opens with an ominous falling minor scale that sets the mood for the work and, coincidentally, preoccupied Beethoven over his whole career, recurring almost identically as late as the finale of the Op. 131 string quartet of 1826. The initial subject group ends on fierce chords for all three instruments interspersed by dramatic silences. A tense theme follows, underpinned by running notes in the viola; it leads into the second theme, in E-flat major, which offers only slight relief from the anxieties of the preceding material. Leaping figures and more dramatic pauses characterize the closing group. The development section is intense, with exciting recurrences of the big chords and one of Beethoven's clever returns to the opening material, here stated by the viola and cello under swirling figuration for the violin, which the composer transforms into a shuddering accompaniment through much of the recapitulation and the short coda.

Although the Adagio con espressione is a generously proportioned moment of repose, its first theme has a touchingly halting quality. But soon the violin stretches out in several luxurious, cadenza-like passages. The contrasting middle section presents a new melody, with all three instruments given independent lines that serve to elaborate the new tune. Beethoven gives the last occurrence of this theme to violin and cello, which the composer makes sing in an unusually high register, displaying a freedom in handling the instrument that's ahead of its time. The coda features shortened violin cadenzas and a lovely, gentle break-up of the opening theme.

Fast and fierce, the scherzo is in three parts. The athletic opening section, which features the opening scramble, is soon followed by sharply accented unison passages of great force. The middle section offers contrast with its mostly chordal textures and lilting rhythm, though its harmonic instability is at once pleasing and unsettling. And there's a witty fade-out of the coda.

The sonata-form finale opens with wiggly triplets leading to a melodic phrase that rises and falls grandly; it bears some resemblance to the finale of Haydn's great G Major String Quartet, Op. 76 No. 1, composed a year or so before this. The second theme is more lyrical, but the composer gives it little breathing room in this fast-paced, dramatic movement. As in the C Minor Piano Trio, Beethoven moves at the end into C major. And again, as in the Op. 1 No. 3 work, the shift to major is achieved subtly and without triumphalism, ending the work quietly, dramatically, mysteriously.

One-offs, Great and Small

Beethoven composed many individual pieces for chamber ensembles: three are important. We'll carefully examine the String Quintet, Op. 29; the Septet for Winds and Strings, Op. 20; and the Quintet for Piano and Winds, Op. 16. And we'll take brief looks at several other works as well.

I mentioned in the last chapter that the C Minor String Trio may be the sleeper among Beethoven's great chamber works, but in fact, it's one of two, the other being the String Quintet in C Major, Op. 29. Like the C Minor Trio, this marvelous work of 1801 is rarely heard but well worth getting to know. Mozart's quintets for two violins, two violas, and cello justifiably rule the roost in this small category: four of the six (K. 515, 516, 593, and 614) are acknowledged to stand among the very greatest of his compositions for any chamber ensemble. The pair by Brahms are relatively popular, at least in recorded versions, as is one of the two by Dvořák. Schubert's justly revered Quintet for Strings, D. 956, of 1828, is for a different ensemble—two violins, one viola, and two cellos. So the obscurity of Beethoven's quintet is both hard to explain and unjust; it has simply fallen between the cracks, even though it's on a par with anything he wrote at this time in his career.

The sound of a string quintet is unquestionably richer than that of the trio. Where there was only one inner voice, there are now three (the second violin and the violas), opening new sonic possibilities. These include freeing the first violin part to soar higher, which Beethoven allows it quite noticeably to do. And of course there are other examples of Beethoven's exploitation of the greater sonority. Finally, the work has a breadth and tranquility all its own, reflected by the opening theme, a shifting idea in steady quarter notes stated by the first violin and tracked below by the cello, with the first viola playing an accompanying figure in eighth notes. A figure in scurrying triplet rhythm follows. The second subject, based on a falling figure for the violins and the first viola, is of great beauty.

It's important to note that that Beethoven casts that second subject in A major, an unusual procedure for the time. Like most of the best composers—including his chief models, Mozart and Haydn—Beethoven constantly flouted academic rules of composition. One rule he chafed at from early on was the requirement of classical sonata structure that a second subject be in the dominant key, which for a work in C major (referred to as the tonic key) would be G major. He grew more interested in using keys a third apart, such as the first subject's C major and the A major of the second, a third down from C major. I cited instances in earlier piano trios where Beethoven wrote second subjects a third away from the tonic key, but it was around the time of this quintet that he began to explore this relationship more intensively and systematically. As Beethoven matured, he applied his own harmonic rules regularly and, as we'll see, to ever more telling effect. His influence on composers (and audiences) who followed is enormous, because he liberated them from the slavish predictability of the tonic-to-dominant rule by moving freely but artfully between keys. Beethoven's renown as an innovator and revolutionary is based as much on subtle but profound alterations such as this as it is on his more obvious expansion of forms, or of turning violent accents into standard musical vocabulary.

You'll note as well how easily Beethoven adapts to his more spacious ensemble. The string trios pose the problem of creating the illusion of more sound than three instruments actually make, which the composer solves, perhaps predictably, by having them all play lots of big chords. But here he can revel in combinations, such as that of the violin playing high in its range and the cello low; there's also a striking passage in the coda where the violins and first viola share a massive trill, four measures long. A new and charming chirping figure for the second violin appears at the start of the recapitulation, and the first subject receives a much more grandiose statement in the development, which the composer later introduces into the recapitulation. The movement's overall proportions and calm affect resemble those of the opening movement of Mozart's Quintet, K. 515, also in C major.

The very beautiful slow movement, operatic in inspiration, opens with a memorable rising melody for the first violin, to which the cello adds a plucked accompaniment and the middle strings a rich harmonic background. This is elaborated luxuriously before a falling phrase signals the approach of the second theme, pitting first violin and cello against each other over shuddering notes for the violas in a hazier harmonic pattern; the cello concludes this group with an eloquent idea elaborated with trills. The third thematic strand consists of a detached motif for all the strings that leads to a powerful stalking figure in the first violin over violent shuddering in the rest of the instruments. Beethoven brings the ideas back in sequence, embellishing and expanding as he proceeds. You'll note, for example, the rich instrumental texture of the second full statement of the opening theme, to which the second violin adds plucked chords and the cello a rowing rhythm beneath. The third theme comes back in fully dramatic posture, with the stalking figure for the first violin leading ultimately to broken notes that sound like a passage from an aria in which a sighing or sobbing effect is sought. In the coda the composer plays with single detached notes, which he scatters gently, with the exception of one loud chord, to the end. The scherzo is a typical excellent example of Beethoven's style for this kind of three-part movement. The cheerful opening tune seems to be constantly pitching forward over ever shifting harmonies. A droning figure for the cellos and second viola add a rustic dance quality. The trio starts with a soaring tune in F major before shifting to a more remote A-flat major, then takes on a more aggressive rhythm to prepare the way for the return of the opening section.

The finale, a thrilling storm in sonata form, is interesting and exciting in every way. The first theme is full of dramatic pauses and a streaking bit of audible lightning for the first violin, while the rolling second subject shows a continual restlessness of harmony and rhythm. But the most unusual aspect of the finale is Beethoven's insertion twice of a slower minuet. Not that the idea of pulling the finale up short this way is original; Mozart did it in several piano concerto finales, albeit to different effect. Beethoven puts the minuet's first appearance in A major, the unusual key of the first movement's second subject, showing his capacity for long-range thinking over the span of a four-movement work of this kind. The second time the minuet shows up, it's right before the climactic final appearance of the first theme and the coda, and this time Beethoven puts it in C major, satisfying our need for the work to end in the tonic key, its harmonic home base.

There's another quintet in C minor, with the tantalizingly high opus number of 104, that's a transcription by Beethoven of the piano trio in the same key, Op. 1, No. 3. The story behind this work is that one Kaufmann, an amateur admirer of the composer, took a stab at the job of transcribing the piece, presenting his weak version to the composer. Beethoven didn't care for Kaufmann's arrangement and decided to make his own. As you might expect, Beethoven's is wonderful, but it is rarely recorded or performed; apparently, most listeners are satisfied with the original version. If you're just getting to know the piano trios, you may have enough to think about, but do keep in mind that the Op. 104 sounds quite different from its parent and is well worth hearing.

Beethoven worked on his Septet in E-flat Major, Op. 20, in 1798–99, premiering it toward the end of the latter year. Well crafted but conventional, the septet achieved great popularity in Beethoven's lifetime, ultimately annoying the composer, who hated to hear it compared favorably to his later, greater, but more challenging music.[1] Nevertheless, there's much to enjoy in this divertimento-like work for clarinet, bassoon, horn, violin, viola, cello, and double bass. Like Mozart's divertimenti, it's cast in six movements, with the first and last featuring impressive slow introductions; in a characteristic change, Beethoven makes the fifth movement a scherzo instead of a second minuet, as Mozart usually did.

The first movement's introductory passage is short but impressive, starting with a powerful rowing figure before moving to an even more striking jogging phrase in detached sixteenth notes for all the instruments. The main body of the movement is based on a sequence of cheerful themes, the first a little four-note tune stated by the violin and the second a more lyrical melody that opens in long-held half notes. The closing theme, which is based on the four-note tune, is first stated by all the strings, then repeated emphatically by the entire ensemble.

Beethoven fits two developments into this spacious movement. The adagio that follows highlights a long and glorious melody, very much in the Italian operatic mode, sung by the clarinet and joined first by the bassoon and then the horn, to which the strings provide a gently rocking background. The violin, followed by the bassoon, then picks up the tune. The violin later covers the melody with more pathos, in a dramatically remote key, but the clarinet recovers it sweetly.

Beethoven took the perky theme of the third-movement menuetto from a piano sonata he had not published, though he treats it more broadly here. The shadowy second section of the trio features, in addition to flourishes for the clarinet and horn, a quieter but nonetheless arresting syncopated passage for the strings. Five variations on a simple two-part theme make up the fourth movement. In the first variation Beethoven displays his fondness for the cello, which he makes sing in its tenor register. The second variation is an amusing scramble for the violin, to which the clarinet contributes elegantly phrased sighs, while the third variation highlights the winds, especially the bassoon, an instrument that's generally relegated to the background. The beautiful fourth variation, in a minor key, has the melody carried in long lines by the three winds while the violin and viola play racing triplets and the two lower strings support the whole structure with pizzicati. The coda has some coy sighs for the clarinet and bassoon, which is trailed by a surprisingly ominous phrase for viola, cello, and bass, before Beethoven relaxes again for the final measures.

The marvelous scherzo is dominated by the sound of the horn, from the skipping opening phrase to the almost constant punctuation it provides in the main portion of the movement, though not the very smooth trio, which features the strings and a light accompaniment by the bassoon. Once again in this passage, Beethoven assigns the melody to the cello, set by the composer in a unusually high register. You'll enjoy the two-note phrases the horn trades with the rest of the ensemble in the movement's outer sections. All Beethoven's scherzos from this era resemble one another in their magnificent rhythmic impetus, and this is among the most enjoyable of the lot.

The finale, a large-scale piece that balances the first movement, opens with a weighty introduction in C minor, in which the horn continues its domination of the ensemble. But the main body of this sonata-form movement is based on the contrasts between a fast, fiddly tune for the strings—regularly interrupted by a falling horn call, akin to the main theme of the preceding scherzo—and an astonishing chorale (a sequence of smooth, hymnlike chords) for the winds, under-pinned by string pizzicati, that looks far into the future, sounding as though it might have been lifted from something by Brahms or Wagner. Beethoven follows this remarkable passage with a long, showy cadenza for the violin before blending the two disparate ideas (the nervous first theme and the dreamy chorale), then guiding them toward a happy conclusion of great delicacy, in which every instrumental strand can be clearly heard.

The last of the important individual chamber works we'll look at is the Quintet for Piano and Winds in E-flat Major, Op. 16, which Beethoven wrote in 1796 and published in 1801. The key signature and instrumentation (oboe, clarinet, horn, bassoon, and piano) of Beethoven's work are identical to those of yet another Mozartean masterwork, K. 452, written in 1784. That Beethoven composed his quintet with Mozart's example in mind is likely but unverified;[2] and Beethoven's quintet, though really fine on its own terms, is not as great as Mozart's, to which it's inevitably compared and which Mozart is on record as considering "the best work I've written in my entire life."[3] Thus it falls into the same category as the string trios and quintets, where Mozart happens to top the charts. The all-time champion com-poser for winds in any case, Mozart's quintet is joyous and of a highly polished beauty, as well as being true chamber music in its balance of the five ensemble parts. Beethoven's resembles a piano concerto, with a brilliant and difficult part for the keyboard and the winds in more subservient roles.

Like Mozart, Beethoven begins his quintet with a slow introduction, his in a stately dotted rhythm, an exaggerated long-short (da-*dum*), played by all the instruments. Beethoven alternates the dotted figure with flourishes and a melodic phrase for the keyboard, then repeated by the winds, in their inimitable, sweet-sour blended tone. This moves into a broader section, with an arpeggio for the piano broken rhythmically between the two hands against the melodic phrase stated earlier; a new, stamping, marchlike figure is traded between the winds and piano, and Beethoven shifts his harmony toward the dominant key of B-flat major. The first theme, stated by the piano, is long (sixteen bars) and divided into four phrases, the first two assertive and the third and fourth with a sighing affect well suited to winds. It's carefully tailored for development. The winds respond immediately, then pass phrases around as the piano busily and virtuosically spins triplets, hammered octaves, and fast passagework. The second theme, meltingly lyrical in character, makes its first appearance in the piano, which is soon joined by the clarinet and bassoon, making it sound even better. Beethoven ends the exposition with a series of themes, the first dashing, the second dreamy, and the third emphatic. It's with the last idea that the composer begins a long development section characterized by triplets for the piano under shifting harmony provided by the winds. The ensemble then dissects the first theme, leading to a long scale for the piano in the expectant B-flat major harmony and finally the recapitulation. The composer pries open the themes, adding repetitions of phrases and a remarkably long trill for the piano, soon followed by the emphatic restatement of a three-note phrase and an extended flourish—really a mini-cadenza—for the piano. The composer gives the horn some exciting material in the coda.

The second movement is a slow rondo based on a very beautiful melody with a prominent falling figure, stated by the keyboard alone. The winds join in rich harmony as the piano takes off with flowing passagework. The first episode features a sad, rising melody for the oboe and bassoon; they're later joined by the clarinet over a nervous keyboard accompaniment. Beethoven drapes the second appearance of the rondo in a profusely florid, sighing figuration for the piano; the second contrasting episode has a magnificent extended solo for horn, accompanied by the piano. The winds take a more active role in the final appearance of the rondo theme, making lyrical interjections throughout. The long coda, which features some tricky writing for the piano, is a meditation on the falling notes of the opening melody.

The finale, a rondo-sonata hybrid, bears little aural resemblance to the closing of Mozart's quintet, but it's still fairly Mozartean. It opens (in the solo piano, again) with what the earlier composer would have called a "hunting" theme—seemingly prime ground for the horn, which was associated in the eighteenth century with hunting music—but except near the final bars, Beethoven declines to give the instrument special treatment. The first episode is a beautiful, lilting passage dominated by the keyboard, which is joined wittily by the bassoon, and it ends with a cadenza for the keyboard. The second episode is a development of the opening idea, adding a sonata-movement aspect to this solid but charming rondo. Phrases overlap excitingly in the final appearance of the rondo theme, and the coda reveals a more ardent side to the good-natured material.

A few stray pieces remain, first the Sextet in E-flat Major for Two Horns and String Quartet, Op. 81b, a cheerful work for another Mozartean ensemble (see, for example, the Divertimento, K. 334) from the mid-1790s published in 1810 with a deceptively high opus number. In a strange conflation of eras and genres, its companion in this middle-period opus is the Piano Sonata No. 26 nicknamed "Les Adieux"—the Farewells. The early sextet is nowhere near the level of that remarkable keyboard work by the mature composer, but it does have its charms. The material is fairly standard hunting-horn stuff, but Beethoven's writing for the brass is ambitious and varied, giving the players little rest. The Sonata in F Major for Piano and Horn, Op. 17, is a lyrical work that's really enjoyable, especially if you listen to the recording by the British French horn virtuoso Dennis Brain, one of the greatest instrumentalists ever recorded. The Op. 17 sonata is interesting too for its structure: it contains a "shadow" slow movement and, typically for Beethoven, a piano part of some difficulty. Finally, there's a Serenade in D Major for Flute, Violin, and Viola, Op. 25, thought to date from 1801. It's a light work in six movements, divertimento-like in character. With the viola acting as the deepest-toned instrument, the sonority is exceptionally bright, and the style is surprisingly rococo for the usually serious and ambitious composer. But Beethoven's craftsmanship even in this uncharacteristic work stays at a high level.

Beethoven and the
String Quartet

The string quartet is the most respected genre of chamber music in which Beethoven worked, and the one where he aimed the highest. Beethoven's place in the history of the string quartet is, with Mozart and Haydn, at its pinnacle.

Thanks to Haydn, the string quartet itself, comprised of two violins, one viola, and one cello, quickly became the musical genre into which composers poured their most careful and studied efforts. The four-movement, sonata-based formats of the symphony and the string quartet are usually identical, but the quartet is less public and showy than the symphony and encouraged composers such as Beethoven to express themselves more intimately than in the public ceremony that an orchestral performance was and still is. Indeed, string quartets were originally often performed in homes, by families or groups of friends; audiences, if any, were incidental. It's important to keep in mind that the market of the day was heavily slanted toward home players or small public performances; music-making was most commonly a private activity for the middle and upper classes, and of course there were no recordings. Beethoven's middle and late quartets are so difficult technically that they require professionals or amateurs of exceptional ability, and so the composer's string quartets received public or semi-public performances; but then, as now, audiences were small and highly dedicated. A large hall, in which the ensemble's relatively small sound can get lost, is not the proper venue for performance of string quartets.

Haydn devised the string quartet in the 1760s, the formative years of the classical era. His inventive genius found the formula for four instruments engaged in a conversational interchange of thematic ideas, and on the practical side, is still easy to gather such an ensemble together. With the eternal exception of Mozart's Divertimento, K. 563, as an ensemble the string trio typically sounds lean, and assembling more than four performers can become an organizational challenge. And the four instrumental parts of a quartet, with its wide tonal range but well-blended string timbres, has the flexibility composers need to play out their ideas without cramping the sound or the ensemble.

Although not chronologically of the same generation, Haydn (born in 1732), Mozart (born in 1756), and Beethoven (born in 1770) make up the first generation of important string quartet composers. No one would dispute that they are also the greatest. Haydn's fertility is unmatched, and an acquaintance with his string quartets is essential for anyone seriously interested in chamber music. Mozart, who first learned from Haydn before developing his own sophisticated quartet style, also requires the serious listener's attention. Interestingly, Haydn may have taken from Mozart, too,[1] employing what he learned from his good friend in the extraordinary quartets he wrote in the decade after Mozart's death in 1791. And of course Beethoven, who studied the quartets of both masters, expanded the genre greatly, though it would not be accurate to call him the greatest of the three Viennese masters. Moreover, the influence of Haydn and Mozart on Beethoven is clear to the very end of his career as a composer of quartets.

Beethoven's quartet writing activity fell (conveniently for musicologists and listeners alike) into the three well-known phases of his creative life. The six quartets of Op. 18, composed between 1799 and 1801, were among the culminating efforts of his early period, as he methodically extended his efforts over the various musical genres, starting with sonatas and variations for piano, then attempting bigger, more important genres when he felt ready. Beethoven's reliance on models by Haydn and Mozart is particularly clear in Op. 18. But these quartets, though well crafted—perhaps even somewhat too carefully crafted—lack the boldness and excitement of the later works. They seem more significant as proving grounds for the composer than they are pleasurable or stimulating for most listeners. If you've never listened to Beethoven's quartets, it's probably best to start with the "Razumovsky" Quartets, Op. 59, and work your way back later to Op. 18.

The next five quartets—the three of Op. 59, Op. 74, and Op. 95—fall into the master's middle period. These represent a huge jump in scope and force, and the personalities of the works are not just bigger, but more radically different from one another. The Op. 59 works, commissioned by the Russian ambassador to the Austrian court, have carried his name, Razumovsky, ever since. They represent a gigantic expansion of size and intensity in Beethoven's quartet writing, much as the Symphony No. 3 (the "Eroica") does in Beethoven's symphonic output, breaking molds and changing musical dimensions forever. The other two middle-period works, which Beethoven composed toward its end, also possess very strong profiles. Op. 74, nicknamed the "Harp" Quartet, is lyrical but utterly quirky. Its closest stylistic cousin is the Piano Trio, Op. 70 No. 2, which we looked at in chapter 6. The Op. 95 quartet is of rare intensity, even for Beethoven, anticipating in its compression and strangeness some aspects of Beethoven's late style, though it was composed only in 1810. (You may recall that the last Sonata for Piano and Violin, Op. 96, of 1812, also looks ahead to the late style, but more in the quality of its lyricism.)

Beethoven went through a phase of low productivity between 1812 and 1816. When his creativity surged again in 1817, he began what's known as his late period, which lasted until his death in March 1827. The products of this phase are diverse in scale, from the vast Ninth Symphony and the *Missa Solemnis* to the more intimate scale of the last three piano sonatas and the tiny Bagatelles for piano, Op. 119 and Op. 126. While it is difficult to generalize about such varied works, Beethoven's late style is notable for displaying musical thinking far in advance of its time, emotional profundity, and a spirituality that forms an unmistakable thread running through one composition after another, in all genres. The five late quartets, written between 1824 and 1826—Beethoven's final works—represent a high point even in this revered composer's output.

The first three late quartets in order of composition are the E-flat Major, Op. 127 (1824–25); the A Minor, Op. 132 (1825); the B-flat Major, Op. 130, along with the *Grosse Fuge*, Op. 133—the Great Fugue—Beethoven's original finale for Op. 130 (1825); the last two are the C-sharp Minor, Op. 131; and the F Major, Op. 135 (both 1826).

(The out-of-sequence opus numbering reflects confusion resulting from the involvement of several publishers.) These five great works show the diversity typical of Beethoven in all his creative periods. All but Op. 135 are conceived on a large scale: Op. 127 is a profound lyrical essay in four long movements; Op. 132, while also fundamentally lyrical, expresses pain and exaltation. The six-movement Op. 130 is the most problematic, with five movements of wildly divergent character, ending either with the mammoth, modernistic Great Fugue or the shorter, more conventional finale Beethoven wrote in late 1826 as a substitute for the fugue. The seven-movement Op. 131 is the composer's most advanced and brilliant work, a virtuoso juggling act in which different styles, forms, and affects are brought into play and miraculously unified. The final work, the cheerful Op. 135, looks back to Haydn and Mozart in its four-movement format and is perhaps the most polished of all Beethoven's compositions.

While an internal diversity marks the late quartets, some unifying elements also exist. Perhaps the most famous is Beethoven's use of related four-note themes in the first movement of Op. 132, where the idea can be plainly heard, in a more attenuated way over the entire span of Op. 131, and in the Great Fugue, which is densely saturated by it from start to finish. While it may be useful to know these exist, your appreciation of the music will not be enhanced by listening for their appearances nearly as much as by paying attention to the big picture.

Because these were Beethoven's last works, swooning commentators have frequently burdened the late quartets with an undeserved valedictory significance. Consider that Beethoven worked on these for a full three years, and that, as you'll see, his struggle to find a form for Op. 130 was still going on when he died. Also, think of the strengths of the last two quartets completed in 1826: Op. 131 is the work of a creative power at absolute high tide, and the sprightly Op. 135 hardly sounds like the work of a dying man. Although periodically ill over his last ten years of his life, Beethoven got sick in December 1826 and died three months later because medicine of the time couldn't save him (perhaps the same pneumonia and diseases of the gastrointestinal system and liver would have killed him even today). But while often ill, he was not a dying man over the three years he worked on the late quartets.

As you might expect, the achievements of Haydn, Mozart, and Beethoven in this realm made life very difficult for composers who followed them. Schubert tried to apply his own style to Beethoven's large scale, with mixed success; his tendency toward repetitiousness and his inability to manage large-scale structures until the very end of his short life results in fervently melodious, often dramatically gripping quartet movements that are loved by all but that unfortunately lack cohesion over the spans of four-movement works. At least Schubert's aim was high, because most other composers cut a more cautious path. The quartets of Mendelssohn, Schumann, and Brahms, for instance, are traditionally styled and attractive, but they come nowhere near the scale and originality of those by the big three. Only in the twentieth century did some find a new way to address the hallowed genre. The single string quartets by Debussy and Ravel adhere to traditional structures but speak convincingly in the composers' individual voices. The two by Leoš Janáček are also strong and characteristically spasmodic. Bela Bartók really gets the credit for reviving the genre with his six, composed over a span of thirty years; each speaks in a different but distinctive voice, and each is full of personality in ways that bring the quartets of the big three to mind. Shostakovich's fifteen string quartets are brilliant works in that master's gloomy, acid-tinged idiom. Those of the Second Viennese School—Arnold Schoenberg, Alban Berg, and Anton Webern—are not popular, but all stretch the boundaries of the genre in their ways. Britten's three are traditional in form but affecting, and Elliot Carter's (five so far), though not for the faint of heart, can be as bracing as they are challenging.

The Early Quartets

9

Most listeners come to love Beethoven through big middle-period works; only afterward do they discover the pleasures of his early and later styles. Suddenly overwhelmed upon hearing the Fifth Symphony, or perhaps the Third, or the Seventh, they eventually learn that the Fourth is fine, and the Second and Eighth quite wonderful, too. If one's love of Beethoven starts with a piano work, it's likely to be the "Waldstein" or "Appassionata," big-boned, powerful sonatas from the middle period, that does the trick; the exploration of the earlier sonatas then turns into a deeply rewarding journey. In the less likely scenario that a chamber work first caught the listener's attention, it might be a powerful piece, such as the "Kreutzer" Sonata, or perhaps a generously lyrical one, such as the "Archduke" Trio; and again, discovering the earlier violin sonatas and piano trios will be a source of great pleasure. If it's one of the "Razumovsky" Quartets that strikes the listener, then the exploration of the other middle-period and late quartets falls quite readily into place.

But this needs to be said: Beethoven's Op. 18 String Quartets—the "early" quartets—probably contain more dull music than any of his important works in any category. Assaults by enthusiastic newbies on Op. 18 typically end in puzzlement and boredom: can these really by the same composer who nearly always thrills? As Beethoven's vehicles in mastering quartet writing technique, they are conservative, even cautious in style, showing little of the boldness that characterizes the ten middle and late quartets. From a stylistic standpoint, Beethoven is somewhat indebted in the Op. 18 quartets to Haydn and Mozart; and the fourth, in C minor, in which he sounds most like the Beethoven we know, has—controversially, as we'll see—been called the weakest of the set. Of course the Op. 18 quartets sound like neither Haydn nor Mozart, but that's not necessarily a plus. At this time in his career, in this medium, Beethoven sounds unsettled, a bit uncomfortable. Still unable to match Haydn's wit and lightness of touch, an unleavened Beethoven copies the intellectual density of Mozart's quartets without Mozart's polish. Wit, delicacy, energy, high finish, and much more will appear abundantly, in Beethoven's own manner, in the middle and late quartets. To look at it another way, in Op. 18 Beethoven surpasses everyone in the first era of quartet composers except Mozart and Haydn, neither of whom he really comes close to. As one critic, the frank, often acerbic Joseph Kerman writes, "There are . . . no master-pieces among the Op. 18 pieces."[1] The high level of Beethoven's output accustoms us to masterpieces, inevitably throwing more workmanlike compositions into the shade. And of course, the opus contains moments and whole movements that are fine; the first, sixth, and perhaps the maligned fourth quartets stand up reasonably well, at least in part. I'll try to make them as interesting as possible. But it's best to approach them without overly high expectations; and probably best too not to listen to more than one in the course of a day.

Beethoven worked on the Op. 18 quartets from 1798 to 1801, when they were published in two installments of three quartets each. They were commissioned by Prince Franz von Lobkowitz, an Austrian noble-man and patron of the composer's and recipient of the dedications of other significant works, perhaps most notably the Symphony No. 3— the mighty "Eroica." The six string quartets of Op. 18 were Beethoven's chief project during these years. The composer's sketchbooks reveal his work on all but the C Minor Quartet (No. 4), revealing his process, and show that he revised them continually. In 1799 Beethoven sent a manuscript of the first version of the F Major Quartet to Karl Amenda, one of his closest friends. Two years later, Beethoven wrote to Amenda, warning: "Be sure not to hand on to anyone your quartet, in which I have made some drastic alterations. For only now have I learned to write quartets."[2] Thus, for Beethoven the experience of working on the quartets had taught him to tighten, cut, and streamline; the original versions all contain more material and thicker ensemble writing than that seen in the revised ones.[3] The sketchbooks, along with documents later found in the Lobkowitz family archive, reveal that the D Major Quartet, published as Op. 18 No. 3, was the first composed, followed by the F Major and G Major Quartets, all in 1799; the C Minor, A Major, and B-flat Major Quartets were finished by 1800, along with major revisions of the F Major and G Major Quartets.[4] The quartets were published in two volumes, in 1801. Beethoven placed the three strongest quartets—the F Major, C Minor, and B-flat Major—in the positions of highest prominence within the opus: that is, first, last, and first in the second group of three as published.

Beethoven considered the F Major Quartet, Op. 18 No. 1, the most important and impressive in the series and clearly spent a great deal of time and effort on its original version. That he returned to the work, revising it thoroughly before publication, reveals his regard and hopes for this ambitious composition as he sent it out into the world. The terse six-note motto that opens the work and permeates the large-scale first movement carries considerable coiled energy. The sketchbook reveals that this easy, almost generic-sounding gesture, with its little turn, took Beethoven nine tries to pin down.[5] The quiet initial statements are followed by two louder ones, then the addition of chords in more ambiguous harmony. The graceful second theme, in the expected dominant key of C major, appears in a rocking rhythm that contrasts with the dynamic first theme. The main theme returns, traded between the first violin and cello. The closing group can be identified by a forceful chord sequence in a remote harmony, preceded by a long silence. Early in the development Beethoven embarks on a fugato passage begun sternly by the cello, which quickly dissolves into a homophonic (melody-driven) version of the first theme for the first violin and a long preparation for the return to the main material, which the full quartet states forcefully. Classical composers rarely introduced new material late in the course of a sonata movement, but in an unusual maneuver Beethoven kicks off the coda by adding a new theme, a powerful rising scale that he then decorates playfully with the turn from the main motto.

Karl Amenda reported that Beethoven had the tomb scene of *Romeo and Juliet* in mind when drafting the slow movement of the quartet, a passionate lament in the Italian vocal style. It opens with a pulsing figure for the lower strings, which the first violin soon joins in a long, affecting melody characterized by hovering steplike motion and decorated with slow turns. The cello, in its high register, takes up the lament, which Beethoven then breaks into decorative patterns and a soothing major-key melody. The development section repeats the opening theme in an angrier tone, and a writhing figure for the cello pulls the harmony back toward the opening key of D minor. The recapitulation blends the sad first statement of the theme with its furious incarnation from the development. Beethoven ends this generously scaled and effective movement gently with a lavishly ornamented version of the opening melody, which he breaks delicately into fragments.

The scherzo, based on a curt theme, is interesting at least in part for the low murmur of its dynamic scheme, where Beethoven's control of soft and very soft sounds is worth noticing. And in contrast, the more rustic trio roars away at a fortissimo. The trio also features some rhythmic condensation that's very striking and advanced. The finale is a big rondo with a development based on Beethoven's scrambling take-off of the principal theme of the finale of Mozart's D Major Quartet, K. 499. This big movement sets a comfortable mood for the end of the work, with some shimmering harmonic shifts and the requisite contrapuntal passages in the development, which, like their companions from the first movement, simply dissolve. The stabbing off-the-beat rhythm of the second episode's theme is strong, and the coda is more passionate than the cheerful material of the movement might lead one to expect.

The G Major Quartet, Op. 18 No. 2 but the third in order of composition, is completely different in character from the large scale and high ambition of the F major work. Beethoven himself wrote in his sketchbook that it's "in a light style, except its finale."[6] Today, the work has a slightly faded charm that may or may not appeal to a first-time listener. The opening is a Haydnesque gesture of a fussy rising scale for the first violin, followed by replies for the full quartet that mimic a polite eighteenth-century-style conversation with striking accuracy. Other thematic elements, including a louder, marchlike figure, have more bite, and as you listen you'll note the way Beethoven separates the ideas by long, distinct pauses, adding an ironic detachment to their presentation and an unpadded quality to the structure. The composer presents the first part of the second theme group in a mincing rhythmic guise, following it with a more fretful tune that once more resembles speech; the theme is also notable for the way the cello chugs busily far below the other strings. In the development section, Beethoven presents detached thematic elements in mock-stern minor keys as well as a brief but beautiful pianissimo sequence in suspension, a rich-sounding method of creating and then resolving a dissonance. A false recapitulation thunders in wittily over churning in the lower strings, and to the end of the movement Beethoven continues to highlight phrases independently, breaking them apart, highlighting eccentric clauses, and setting them in oppositional dialogue rather than combining them. He ends this fine movement with a coy exchange based on one of the first conversational ideas. The slow movement, which also starts somewhat fussily with a long, rich melody of the sort Beethoven could churn out by the ream, seems inferior in inspiration to the opening. It does, however, contain a surprise: a rushing, scherzo-like middle section that breaks the movement apart formally, moving it into an unanticipated region that's not visionary, just different. The slow melody, tired and a bit trite, comes back, lavishly decorated. The swift central section seems to have been a late idea, because it does not appear in the composer's sketches.[7]

The witty scherzo, a cousin to some in the contemporary piano sonatas, is built on a scampering figure. In the trio Beethoven offers up the ghost of the menuettos that formerly held sway as third movement of ambitious classical-era instrumental works by himself, Mozart, and Haydn. The last movement is a bit heavier, at least in its demands on the players, but continues in the humorous mood of the first and third movements; it is also rich in clever contrapuntal devices. A collapsing rhythmic figure for the whole ensemble portends a disaster that the affect of this movement will not permit; though he brings the figure back twice again, Beethoven playfully lets its menace evaporate.

As noted, the D Major Quartet, third in published order, was the first of the Op. 18 set to be composed. Though a well-made work, its mild manners make it less likely to hold the attention of a first-time listener than others of these six. You may want to consider returning to it after getting acquainted with the First, Fourth, and Sixth Quartets; even the Second Quartet—the G Major we just looked at—has a stronger profile. The last movement, a tarantella that wants to be wild but goes on too long, is its weakest.

The first movement opens with an extremely gentle theme that rises the interval of a seventh (the most expressive in the classical composer's vocabulary) sounding like a sigh. Eighth notes passed from the violins down to the viola loosen the melodic flow. The second group begins with a spunkier theme recognizable for its scampering triplets followed by sharp off-the-beat accents in a harmonic setting that teeters appealingly between major and minor. The third group starts with a pulsing theme for the full quartet into which the composer continues with the syncopated accents from the first thematic group. Detached chords, vigorously stated by the full ensemble, are the most memorable element of the closing group. The development begins with the first theme, now played by the first violin in D minor; this opens a fairly predictable sequence in which Beethoven breaks his themes into fragments while weaving expertly through a number of keys and building tension by tightening the rhythm and steadily raising the volume. He ends the section with a vehement C-sharp major chord, thundered out in shuddering triplets, that's probably the boldest idea in the work; it's certainly the most striking when you hear it. This leads cleverly into the restatement of the quiet opening idea and the recapitulation.

The slow movement is based on a heartfelt tune, very richly stated by the full group, that sounds like a song or hymn, not an aria, and seems German rather than Italian in its melodic syntax and harmonic support. Formally, it's a rondo-sonata hybrid at a moderately slow tempo with two episodes, the first an elfin idea in which the instruments play sparkling detached notes with the first violin high above. The composer decorates the second appearance of the rondo theme with great skill. But, remarkably, as in the first movement, he instructs the quartet to thunder the theme out, twice, in loudly repeated sixteenth notes just before the coda, in which he delicately disassembles the melody. The third movement is a scherzo, but the composer omits a title, simply giving the tempo indication *allegro*. It's unusual structurally: the opening strain is repeated in the normal fashion, but Beethoven marks the D minor trio as *minore*, and then the return of the opening section, which is back in D major, *maggiore*—major. He also has to write out the third part of the movement because it's not a literal repeat of the opening section. The material is fairly standard for Beethoven in scherzo mode, if a bit gentler than normal to go along with the more contained mood of this quartet. The opening part is characterized by off-the-beat accents and frequent, deliberate hesitations. The central section features the passing cloud of a minor key and more insistent syncopations. But the ensemble writing remains smooth throughout.

The finale is a tarantella—the familiar jumpy Italian dance—in sonata form. Beethoven composed a few such finales, of which this is probably the weakest. In 1802, with five crucial years of development behind him, Beethoven wrote a polished specimen to close the piano Sonata No. 18 in E-flat Major, Op. 31 No. 3; and of course, the "Kreutzer" Sonata's last movement (pp. 37–38), more rhythmically varied, is a far more effective example as well. Tarantella finales are far from easy to carry off, as the repetitious pounding of the da-*dum*-da-*dum* rhythm can quickly become tiresome, and the mood of gaiety, as here, seems forced. Additionally, this theme has an unfortunate resemblance to the "Mexican Hat Dance" we've all heard as the background to cartoons and commercials on television—no fault of Beethoven's, of course. It's put together skillfully enough, though, and the composer brings off some interesting contrasts of sonority between the high first violin and the other strings playing low. In a paradoxical touch, he also contrives to end this supposedly wild movement quietly, surprising first-time listeners who may expect all that furious fiddling and scraping to end with thunderous chords. The influence of this movement on Schubert, who concluded three important mature compositions (the "Death and the Maiden" and G Major String Quartets and the C Minor Piano Sonata) with tarantellas was enormous, though not necessarily salutary. With an irony that's perhaps a bit heavy-handed, Schubert turns at least two of them into "dances of death," ending these serious works in nightmarish fashion; but for some listeners all three finales run on to excess. (The last movement of the G Major Quartet is more ambiguous, but also quite long.)

The C Minor Quartet, fourth in the set, has long been the problem child among the six. Unlike its companions in Op. 18, the work has no sketches that have turned up. This fact, along with circumstantial evidence and a few debatable stylistic clues, led one critic (Hugo Riemann)[8] to speculate that the quartet was of earlier origin than its peers, tossed in and hurriedly updated a bit by Beethoven perhaps because he needed one more composition to get to six, which was Haydn's usual number for publication. Some later critics, such as Barry Cooper and Lewis Lockwood,[9] have disagreed, pointing out that there's no hard evidence at all that the C Minor Quartet is of earlier origin than the rest. And it does seem unlikely that Beethoven, the proud perfectionist, would toss something he considered inferior into his most important compositional effort to that point.

Joseph Kerman's *The Beethoven Quartets* (1966) is an indispensable study of these works. Kerman takes a modified view as to the date of the C Minor Quartet's composition. He perceives the unusual second movement as contemporary with the rest of Op. 18 while pointing out the composition's rough spots and weaknesses, of which there are plenty—as there are in all the Op. 18 quartets. Obviously Kerman's opinion is his own; and if you don't know Beethoven's quartets, you will want to acquaint yourself with them all. Kerman is also exceptionally sensitive to what he (along with many others) sees as the composer's chief flaw: his lack of subtlety, which Kerman hears in abundance in Op. 18 No. 4. At all events, Kerman deserves credit for calling out a weakness where he sees it.

If you've never heard the early quartets and you're listening in numerical sequence, there's a fair chance the C Minor will strike you favorably, especially after the pallid Second and Third Quartets. Right from the start it sounds more like the Beethoven we love, and the work has an interesting format. For one thing, it lacks a slow movement: a scherzo at a moderate speed in dance rhythm takes its place, followed by a grim menuetto. The composer deployed identical structures for other important instrumental works, including the piano Trio in E-flat Major, Op. 70 No. 2 (pp. 60–64), and the Symphony No. 8. You've also heard other fiery dramas in his signature key of C minor, such as the Sonata for Piano and Violin, Op. 30 No. 3; the Piano Trio, Op. 1 No. 3; and the String Trio, Op. 9 No. 3. While we may agree with Kerman that this quartet is not as fine as those compositions, it does offer some pleasures of its own, just the same.

The first movement opens directly with the first theme, sung by the first violin in its lower range. Intense and thick with passion over a throbbing accompaniment by the cello, it is richly harmonized by the middle strings. It's also marked almost immediately by sharply accented notes—*sforzandi*—that add to the tense atmosphere. The melody soars anxiously before ending in a storm of huge chords. The most notable element of the second theme group is a melody in G major that, except for its beseeching manner, closely resembles the opening theme. The closing thematic group consists of two themes of great rhythmic impetus and massive chords to round it out. These are expanded in the development, which also gives the cello a moment of glory as it sings the pleading melody high in its alto register. The coda is short but very forceful.

As noted, Beethoven substitutes a playful scherzo for a slow movement. It looks ahead to the far greater scherzo of the F Major Quartet from Op. 59 to follow: both are based on a rhythm stated in soft staccato notes at the outset. The effect is that of an elfin dance, and there are many subtleties of rhythm and instrumentation to be gained by listening carefully (and following the music in the score, if you can). That said, there are no explosions in this dainty movement, and its effect is contained, even muted. Its unusual placement creates a striking contrast with the serious opening movement, altering the balance and lightening the tone of the whole composition. How well it suits an overall scheme for the work is uncertain. The menuetto is a mordant dance in name only, reclaiming some of the opening movement's darkness of affect. Stabbing accents of the material in the outer sections recall the first movement's textures; and the composer introduces a slight but interesting irregularity of structure, requiring that the repeat of the opening material after the strange murmuring of the trio be taken at a faster tempo than in its first statement. The increase in speed ratchets up the tension and prepares the way for the quick tempo of the finale.

The finale is a rondo with a descending main theme in blustery eighth notes and a decidedly gypsy flavor. The first episode offers one of the few moments of repose in this turbulent work, while in the second the composer introduces the rumbling triplets with which he will end the work. The third appearance of the rondo theme features an ominously sinking bass line and more furious fiddling before Beethoven briefly lightens the sound with a shift to G major, but he ends the work with a wild prestissimo coda in C minor that's emphatic rhythmically but less certain harmonically, as it drifts toward C major in an ambiguous ending that resembles others from his early C minor compositions.

The Quartet in A Major, the fifth in the Op. 18 set, is one of the less memorable of the group–another, along with the second and third, that you may want to take in after listening to its stronger companions. It's loosely modeled on Mozart's String Quartet in A Major, K. 464, which Beethoven admired, going so far as to copy it out in his own hand.[10] I've had to point out Beethoven's inferiority to Mozart in his works in several genres—string trios and wind quintets in particular—and here's one more case, although the last. Beethoven's A Major Quartet comes nowhere close to the mature Mozart's extraordinary work, which you should listen to right away in case you've never heard it. Beethoven's imitation of Mozart's masterwork is limited chiefly to the key and the ordering of the four movements, where, like Mozart, he places the menuetto as the second movement and a set of variations as a moderately slow third. There's also one point in the variations where Beethoven pays tribute to Mozart by imitating—albeit coarsely—a catchy, drumlike passage for cello in Mozart's work. Like the G Major and D Major Quartets (Op. 18 Nos. 2 and 3), the A Major will probably sound relatively unappealing on first and second hearings, but it has a few attractive moments. The second-movement menuetto, though unassuming, is probably the most polished of the minuets and scherzos in Op. 18.

Beethoven's presentation of his rather composite thematic material is striking for its diversity. The opening theme, for example, consists of four ideas: first a vigorous, rising theme, then a lyrical idea in a skipping rhythm stated high up by the first violin. Next comes a fiddly motto, the chief element of which is a scale, and finally another rising figure, this one marked by trills. After a pause, the second theme, another skipping theme (typical for the 6/8 meter in which the movement is set), appears, but lower down and more crisply articulated. The closing theme turns the scalar figure into a longer run. A pause separates the first and second themes, and Beethoven builds other clear breaks into the exposition. The material is attractive and the pace brisk, but the overall effect might strike you as just a bit disjointed. The development has some nice writing for the cello, and Beethoven turns the fiddly fourth idea of the opening group into a giggling figure.

The menuetto is a simple, charming, and well-made specimen that's also a good example of the basic ABA form typical of these movements. The violins introduce the opening strain (the A section), and they are soon joined by the viola and cello in a relaxed and gracious dance that bears only the most general resemblance to Mozart's and Haydn's. The trio—the B filling to the ABA sandwich—is made up of two short sections. The first, only eight bars long, is marked by droning figures and off-the-beat accents for the cello and resembles a rustic dance. The second portion of the trio is a longer, slightly smoother passage. Its character bridges the gap between the country dance and the suave minuet, though the syncopations continue through its entire brief but charming length. As is customary in these movements, the A section is then replayed without repeats.

The third movement, a set of variations on a lyrical theme, is the weakest part of Op. 18 No. 5. For starters, the theme is melodically bland and so chastely diatonic (meaning consonant), without even a whisper of dissonance or chromatic coloring, that we may tire of it even before it has been fully stated. Beethoven builds the contrapuntal first variation from the bottom up: the cello begins the chugging statement of the idea, now presented in a march rhythm, followed by the viola, the second violin, and finally the first violin. In the second variation, the melody is presented in detached notes decorated by triplets; in the third, perhaps the most interesting, the lower strings cover the theme under an accompaniment by the violins in fast notes that hover and shimmer. It looks ahead to the motionless effects to which Beethoven would return later in his career, and it probably influenced Schubert as well. The composer compresses the theme and introduces chromatic slips (finally!) into the texture in the fourth variation, distantly antici-pating one of the remarkable variations in the Op. 131 quartet. In the fifth variation, however, Beethoven shreds the delicate mood he just conjured with a vulgar march in which the middle strings roar out the melody as the violin trills loudly above and the cello bumps along far below. It's hard to know whether the master is putting us on by shoving mock real-world music against more refined, interior material, *à la* Mahler, or simply viewed the march as an acceptable take-off on the theme, but either way it's an awfully jarring moment. Yet he does take the marching rhythm down effectively in an unofficial sixth variation that serves as a long coda to this very lumpy movement.

The finale, however, is interesting and well executed. It's a sonata movement based on a rattling, rather modest four-note idea of the kind that in Beethoven's hands (or Mozart's, or certainly Haydn's) yields surprising dividends, its very neutrality offering the composer broad possibilities for development. The radiant second theme, made up of smooth chords, resembles a chorale in its long-held chordal character. And the closing group features a figure for the first violin that scampers playfully upward. The development contains much contrapuntal material, but the most pleasing passage features mixed textures for the four strings, with the violins playing legato, the viola in pizzicato, and the cello executing its falling figure in a crisp staccato. The ending, too, is effective, as the strings reach up to exhale a huge, happy sigh. The A Major Quartet is decidedly a mix of quite good in the second and fourth movements and inexplicably weak in the third-movement variations.

The sixth and last quartet of the set, in B-flat major, behaves similarly, albeit with different peaks and low points. The first two movements sound a bit flat, but the scherzo and particularly the finale, without doubt the single most remarkable movement in all of Op. 18, reach far higher planes. The opening of the work is promising enough, with an assertive and energetic turn followed by a more lyrical broken chord in a rising pattern, setting a cheerful, somewhat rustic mood. When you listen, pay attention to the dynamics: the composer repeatedly marks notes *fp* (*fortepiano*), a direction that tells the players to attack the note loudly, then drop the volume, giving the music a less aggressive effect. Beethoven follows this solid material with a transitional passage whose bland formality looks back to Haydn, without the benefit of that master's deflating wit. The second theme, however, is good: a rocking sequence undermined by continual harmonic shifts that flicker between its home key of F major and a dangerous F minor that hints at greater depth of feeling. Here's another theme that likely impressed Schubert:

the second theme of the opening movement of his G Major Quartet, Op. 161, strongly resembles Beethoven's. The generally unimpressive development features dullish contrapuntal passages, but Beethoven opens up with the relaxed and thoughtful phrases harmonized with the dominant (D major here) chord, which lead to the recapitulation. Overall the movement suffers from a lack of harmonic movement that's unusual for the normally adventurous Beethoven.

In the second movement, the first violin presents a fairly simple but arching lyrical theme in two parts, varies it with a carefully with a dotted figure for viola and cello, then offers a contrasting middle part opened by a pianissimo passage that's mysteriously unharmonized. The middle section is superficially more expressive, yet without actually expressing a great deal. The return of the main theme after the middle section is encrusted with all the ornamentation that the themes have picked up along the way and then some. Though smoothly assembled, the music is not particularly affecting.

With the scherzo and the finale, Beethoven makes his greatest leap in quality and force. Both movements overflow with the high imagination and indisputable quality lacking in the rest of Op. 18. And the finale, which, unusually, carries the title "La Malinconia"—melancholy—is the single most original passage in Op. 18. Beethoven gives the scherzo (CD Track 4) its unsettling quality by means of a series of sophisticated rhythmic tricks. Before you listen, you should be aware that he writes the piece in a standard-looking 3/4 time signature, which means a steady three beats to the bar, but on paper the music looks, and often sounds, like 6/8, a compound meter that has many rhythmic faces. When you listen to the opening phrase (through 0:17), pay attention to the off-the-beat accents and the hanging endings of the clauses within the phrase (0:09 and 0:17). The second phrase contains more disruptions, including the interplay between the violins and the lower strings from 0:24, which function in 3/4, while the violins sound like 6/8—but everyone is off the beat. You'll hear the syncopated avalanche starting at 0:30 repeated at 1:14. The stabbing accents for the first violin in slightly different rhythmic guises starting at 0:46 are yet another example of the composer's daring in this forward-looking passage. The second section is repeated starting at 1:01. The short trio, which begins at 1:45, is slightly more regular overall, though you'll notice sharply accented notes for all the instruments throughout. An exceptionally vehement passage at 2:25 leads back to the opening section, which is repeated starting at 2:30; note Beethoven's comical insistence on ending with the same unpolished hanging phrase from before.

Beethoven's application of a title to a movement in an abstract work was highly unusual. "La Malinconia" tells us that what follows is a character piece. His equally exceptional instruction tells the performers that the slow, forty-four-bar introduction to the last movement is "to be played with the greatest delicacy." The passage begins with a meditative phrase in B-flat major for the violins and viola that ends with a turn sounding like a sigh, to which the second violin, viola, and cello reply in deeper tones; they, too, end with a sigh. But into the harmony of the turn Beethoven injects a disruptive harmonic shift, a note that leads in just a few bars to obsessive repeats of the turn, ripe with pungent dissonances, which lead in turn to distant keys. Beethoven repeats the opening idea, but now in B major, remote from the B-flat major of the opening bars. (The names of the two tonalities look close, but to the ear they're far apart.) Now comes an openly sorrowful phrase that anticipates the short but melodically potent sixth movement of Op. 131, which also leads into the finale of that quartet. The turns dominate the texture from this point, with the cello assuming the burden of the sigh far below as the other strings, particularly the first violin, reach higher and higher. There's one last iteration of the opening phrase, as the main body of the finale, a *ländler*—the lilting precursor to the waltz— begins without pause. While this gently rocking dance obviously offers much contrast with the introduction, it's not overly cheerful, either, with minor-key inflections that may be decorative but add to its rather subdued affect. And you'll be struck by the return of "La Malinconia" about two-thirds of the way (around six minutes' playing time) into the movement. The interruption is only about forty-five seconds, with the *ländler* picking up again, only to be interrupted for one more brief statement of the "Malinconia" theme. And there's a final reflective slowdown, though this time of the dance alone, right before the short coda, in which the music races madly to its end.

This wonderful movement, the best but least characteristic in Op. 18, seems to breathe a different air from the rest of the set, looking far ahead in its structure and content. It boasts a few important cousins in the master's output, including the first and last movements of the Piano Sonata No. 17, popularly known as the "Tempest," composed in 1802. The themes of the sonata's and the quartet's finales are quite similar, though the sonata is tragic and mysterious in tone; and its opening movement shares with the quartet's finale a free and irregular structure in which slow introductory material returns quite unexpectedly later in the movement. And before either, the first movement of the more famous "Pathétique" Sonata, Op. 13, displays a comparable structural boldness. Beethoven's greatest blending of two movements of different, even disparate tempos and moods in a finale must be the slow movement and fugue that end the Piano Sonata in A-flat Major, Op. 110, of 1821–22; "La Malinconia" prefigures that high achievement of two decades later. One may also hear echoes of this dance theme in that of the great finale of the A Minor Quartet, Op. 132, of 1825. Kerman's mild complaint that "*La Malinconia* does not really seem to approach melancholy," when compared to Beethoven's later skill in portraying sorrow,[11] is correct but gives the composer too little credit for his accomplishment here while comparing it unfairly to some of the greatest music he ever conceived. Whether or not one agrees that the movement lacks real depth of feeling, few would dispute its technical excellence or deny the pleasures listening to it offers.

The piano sonatas provide listeners with one more work for string quartet, a transcription of the Sonata in E Major, Op. 14 No. 1. This fine, relatively modest sonata from the late 1790s was transcribed for string quartet in 1801 or 1802.[12] In this era the expanding middle class took its music seriously, and everyone played an instrument, be it piano, violin, viola, or cello. The E Major Sonata, a relatively easy one by Beethoven's standards, was aimed at the amateur market, and when asked for something for these domestic musicians Beethoven decided to transcribe the work himself rather than leave the job to a hack; the result is a very charming second look at the sonata's material, so idiomatic for string quartet that it's more reinterpretation than simple transcription. First of all, Beethoven recast the piece in F major—not

necessarily an easier key for string players, but one that better allowed
the low C strings of the viola and cello to be used.[13] He also made
many thoughtful changes to the voicing and placement of the parts,
including adding and removing material, so that it sounds as though
it were composed for quartet rather than the piano. But both versions
are really fine, and surely it's best to get to know both. There are many
fine recordings of the piano version (I tend to rely on Schnabel's and
Goode's), but just a few for the string quartet version; those by the
Tokyo and the Kodály String Quartets are terrific.

The "Razumovsky" Quartets, Op. 59

Five years separate the Op. 18 quartets from Beethoven's next set of three, written in 1806, published the following year, and nicknamed for the patron who commissioned them. The intervening years had been among the composer's most productive. Among other works, he had composed the Second and Third Symphonies; the latter, the "Eroica," limns one of the great stylistic boundaries in his own—and musical—history. He also wrote the first version of his only opera, titled *Leonore*, which would later become *Fidelio*. Other works from this flood-tide period include the Third and Fourth Piano Concertos; the Violin Concerto; ten piano sonatas, including the "Moonlight," the "Waldstein," and the "Appassionata"; the important Op. 34 and Op. 35 piano variations; six violin sonatas, from Op. 23 through Op. 47, therefore including the "Spring" and the "Kreutzer"; and the String Quintet, Op. 29.

During this phase of epic productivity, the composer moved from the final products of his early period—the Op. 18 string quartets and the Second Symphony—and into the full grandeur of his middle-period style, which would last through 1812. Beethoven seems to have willed the change in his style from his own restless version of the high classical to something bigger in scale and even more dramatic. The music of this best-known and most popular phase in the master's career, with its overt power and often violent affect, is what typically first grabs the attention of the first-time listener, who, on hearing one of its manifestations, finds it hard to conceive of anything sounding so magnificent. What makes this phase even more astonishing is the knowledge of Beethoven's dreadful personal circumstance, chiefly his deepening deafness, which became public knowledge and led him, in 1802, to consider suicide. Yet even the incomplete list of works above is notable for its high energy and even joy, with remarkably few that express gloom.

Taken separately or as a group, the three string quartets of Op. 59—No. 1 in F major, No. 2 in E Minor, and No. 3 in C Major—stand alongside the "Eroica" as the greatest and most significant works of the first part of Beethoven's middle period, equally important landmarks in his career. Like the Symphony No. 3, their length (which in the case of the F Major Quartet is about forty minutes) nearly doubles that typical of Haydn's, Mozart's, or those of Beethoven's own Op. 18, opening musical structures to greatly augmented spans. While the energy they express is Beethoven's own wild brand, it's not without precedent in works by his predecessors. But the expansion of the pieces is something entirely new and revolutionary, after which Western music has never been the same; as Kerman points out, the enormous dimensions of Wagner's operas and Mahler's symphonies could not have been possible without Beethoven's breaking ground for them in these quartets.[1] And yet they remain true to the disciplines of the string quartet and the nature of chamber music: "these quartets are interior monologues addressed to a private self whose emotional states comprise a variegated tapestry of probing moods and sensations."[2]

Their commissioner and dedicatee, Count Andrei Razumovsky, was the Russian ambassador to the Austrian court, resident in Vienna. A man of high rank and ostentatious wealth, Razumovsky was also a music lover and violinist who played well enough to manage some of the easier second violin parts, but who also had the sense to let a professional take over when new, more difficult material like that of the Op. 59 quartets was to be played. As a tip of the hat to Razumovsky's homeland, an ally of Austria against Napoleon, Beethoven worked Russian themes into the first two quartets. The composer finished these three huge, complex works over the course of just a few months in the summer of 1806. First played in public in 1808 by the Schuppanzigh Quartet, which Razumovsky also backed, they were correctly deemed difficult and treated by reviewers with careful respect, if not much initial enthusiasm. Sensible and forward-looking members of the Viennese music-loving public had already learned not to jump to conclusions about Beethoven's new efforts, knowing that they were ahead of their time and often exceptionally challenging.

Like Haydn and Mozart, Beethoven tried to vary the character of compositions in a set intended for publication: whatever their weaknesses, even the Op. 18 quartets are quite different from one another. And so, to an even greater degree, are their three successors of Op. 59. We cannot pin works as tremendous as these three string quartets down to a single affect or style, but certain observations apply. Both the F major work that opens the set and the E minor one that follows are lyrical dramas; in the first quartet, the master works on an immense scale and in a mood of Olympian calm. In the E minor work Beethoven is tense, inward-looking, with contraction often taking the place of the first quartet's huge musical vistas, though its slow movement is certainly broad and grandly proportioned. And in the third work, which is in the bright and neutral key of C major, Beethoven looks back almost continually at the compositional manners of Haydn and Mozart, with a powerful slow introduction leading into a cheerful opening movement, a menuetto rather than a scherzo, and a fugal finale of wild momentum and high polish. The tone of this final quartet in the set, which the first listeners found the easiest to grasp, seems ironic, while its very beautiful slow movement sounds like nothing else Beethoven wrote.

There's so much great music in the string quartets from this one through the last (Op. 135) that selecting illustrative movements for the CD that accompanies this book was a challenge; but there was never any question that the first movement of the F Major String Quartet, Op. 59 No. 1, had to be included (CD Track 5). Its eleven-minute length takes up a significant portion of the disc, but the movement represents so crucial a page of Beethoven's work for chamber ensemble, as well as one of the clearest examples of the breakthrough in his stylistic development, that it had to be included.

It was unusual, though not unprecedented, for the cello to present the rising opening theme, which you hear right at the start, accompanied by a steady pulse of eighth notes played by the second violin and viola. Beethoven instructs the cello to play *mezzo-forte*, or moderately loud, while the other two instruments play softly. You can immediately feel the excitement in the music. Both Haydn and Mozart presented material in a similar way in string quartets of their own, but perhaps the example that offers clearest precedent is Mozart's String Quintet in C Major, K. 515, which opens with the cello rising from its lowest register to state the first theme of the movement against throbbing eighth notes for the second violin and the two violas, to which the first violin makes its reply; the breadth of Mozart's theme and structure surely had its effect on Beethoven's thinking here, but unlike in the early quartets he is now up to the task of managing material of comparable breadth over the course of a far-flung plan. He also had his own way with excited pulsing accompaniments like this one, which he took to a new level of intensity. The whispered accompaniment to the opening theme of the "Eroica" Symphony, and above all, the throbbing opening of the "Waldstein" Sonata, where the theme is actually embedded in the quick notes, are other potent examples.

Beethoven transfers the first theme to the first violin (0:13), ending on a series of massive F major chords, emphatically stated. The composer reconciles excitement, in the shape of the steady flow of eighth notes, with tranquility by remaining in the home key (F major) for an unusually long period. Notice, too, that the cello's theme consists of a number of separable segments, including the rising quarter notes and the falling eighth notes, that Beethoven will break apart and develop over the course of the movement. The next element of the opening thematic group is a series of brisk, detached chords in a sharp rhythmic profile, followed by a contrasting idea based on smoothly tied figuration (0:47), played first by the violins, then by the lower instruments. At 1:00 the opening idea returns, decorated by triplets; then another detached figure (1:20) is introduced by the cello and passed around. This is the final element of the first thematic group, and all told it's a lot of material to take in. The splendid and richly harmonized melody that follows (1:35) is the second theme; its broad lyricism contrasts with the high energy of the opening material. Beethoven concludes this group with another idea marked by trills played high up by the first violin (1:46), with triplets of a tidal sweep taking over afterward (around 2:00). These lead unexpectedly to a sequence of icy chords in remote harmonies (2:16) that bear no resemblance to anything else and invoke a mood of detachment. Such an idea is common enough in Beethoven, but this particular manifestation of it is exceptionally strange, as though an unknown outsider has joined a congenial family gathering. Beethoven resumes the opening idea at 2:23 and again in its original position at 2:45, as if he's developing it, even though this is the final passage of the exposition.

Now, instead of following the standard classical-era procedure of repeating the exposition, Beethoven plunges directly into the development (around 3:00) although he does not make the boundary absolutely clear. This section begins with a breaking of the main theme, the triplets, and the eighth notes into new positions and harmonies (3:02), followed by an expanded version of the icy chords (3:48). Beethoven then embarks on a prolonged meditation on the opening theme, emphasizing the first four notes and wandering through many keys as the first violin decorates thoughtfully and often very high in its range up to 4:50. At that point an earnest-sounding fugato begins, which proceeds somewhat stormily before heading into the slowly falling chords (5:27) that end it. Again, a reflection of the opening idea, here decorated by more excited triplets, leads to an expectant moment in which Beethoven tricks us into thinking we're heading back to the opening, but instead he presents the second, rhythmically incisive idea in the home key of F major (6:18), then summons the longed-for first theme from underneath (6:37).

Apart from a sense of homecoming that hearing the opening theme in the tonic key implies, the dry term "recapitulation" suggests that the return is straightforward. But for Beethoven, as for Haydn and Mozart before him, the recapitulation functions more as a second development, with expansion and reexamination of all the material. And this already long movement is a fine example of his continuous tinkering with his themes. Right away (around 7:00) you can hear the violin line extended and cast into minor keys. Beethoven here omits the rhythmic figure but extends the flowing idea from the opening group considerably (7:30). At 8:00 the viola takes over the ripe second theme as the first violin embroiders it with triplets. The icy chords come back at 8:40, followed by a tension-building passage backed with powerful rhythmic support from the cello. This leads to a grand climax based on the first theme that fully upholds the movement's dynamism (9:05). The long coda, kicked off by triplets (9:40), allows the composer space for one more thematic incarnation as the first violin soars tranquilly first to a high C (10:09), the dominant pitch in the key of F, and then to the majestic concluding chords, which emphatically stress the home key.

Beethoven solved the problem of how to follow this spectacular sonata movement by writing one of his greatest scherzos. Its playing time, only about a minute shorter than that of the first movement, precludes its presence on the CD, but make sure to listen to it as soon as possible. You'll never forget this brilliantly witty essay in musical comedy even after a single listening. The compressed thematic material and the sequence of discrete events Beethoven develops in this tonal mosaic differs utterly from its predecessor's broad themes and grand architecture. The form seems to be an expanded scherzo and trio upon which Beethoven imposes a sophisticated sequence of keys and some sonata-like aspects in the way the themes are combined and developed,[3] devised by the composer solely for this movement. Its highly individual character is hard to describe, though; one really needs to hear it, and following along in a score will surely help. In addition to the knocking of the opening theme, there's a bland, mincing reply; the third element is a more lyrical waltzlike theme, but all are very short. From these slender materials Beethoven conjures a universe of wit and color. At one point he blends the two opening ideas into a thunderous dance that seems amusingly climactic in the context of this movement's contained expressive range; another is a complex syncopated phrase of tied rhythms in which melody stops and only gentle shifts of harmony color the motion of the instruments, all underpinned by the rocking of the cello; the beginning of the coda sounds like a clock that's winding down. You'll hear, too, that rests, pauses, and a few longer silences carry considerable expressive weight.

The scherzo begins unforgettably with the cello rapping out a distinctive rhythm (short short–long long–short short–long long–shortshortshortshortshortshort–*long*) on a single note (B-flat) so that it sounds like drumming. This extraordinarily advanced idea of giving percussive material to a string instrument—anticipating Debussy and Stravinsky—so offended one of the first cellists to play it that he supposedly threw his score on the floor and stamped on it.[4] Beethoven builds this movement by subjecting the tiny scraps of thematic material he doles out to countless hilarious alterations, whether melodic, harmonic, instrumental, or rhythmic (which is his primary tool here). He carefully gauges shifts of tempo, and the relatively few loud outbursts are closely managed as well. Here Beethoven shows all the subtlety at his disposal, and you'll hear how he develops something that starts so unpromisingly into a profoundly satisfying ten-minute movement, tickling the attentive listener mightily all the way through. Haydn wrote movements that are equally playful and witty, but none on this scale.

The third movement, marked *adagio molto e mesto*—very slow and sad—is cut to the same enormous scale as the first two movements. Beethoven speaks in tragic accents, employing the passionately declaimed Italian vocal style, assembling in a sequence of long, mostly sorrowful melodies. One may look back at the slow movement of the first F Major Quartet, Op. 18 No. 1, for the ancestry of this complex lament and see as well how far the composer came in the seven years between the composition of the two works. The first violin sings out the beautiful but tragic first theme, which the cello then picks up in its alto register over a rich accompaniment by the rest of the ensemble. The cello and first violin also carry the second theme, a long-limbed but equally sorrowful melody that ends in a weeping figure. The long-limbed melody is sung in a not overly consoling major incarnation to a more rapidly flowing accompaniment that develops into a steady plucked sequence for the cello. Finally, the first violin takes up a new, more comforting melody over a shimmering figure for the viola where the composer plays with the paradox of short notes in a slowly changing harmony that seem to hover motionlessly. The melody soars ecstatically in the violin, tracked grandly far below by the viola and cello in a striking, widely spread sonority that Beethoven liked and applied often. Beethoven accompanies the return of the opening melody with a profusion of string sounds, from the legato of the first violin as it carries the tune to the hovering figures of the second violin and viola and the pizzicato of the cello far below. The second melody returns, now sung by the cello followed by the first violin as the composer works the weeping figuration back into this busy ensemble. The coda is based on the opening idea, but a cadenza-like passage for the first violin over shifting major-key harmonies changes the tone, setting the stage for the genial finale.

The first movement was a lyric drama on a grand scale, the second a gnomic scherzo, also long. The third movement was a dirge—also of huge proportions. The finale assumes another posture altogether and, while hardly short, is a bit leaner in its proportions; it is certainly relaxed in its tone. Here Beethoven introduces the Russian element he promised his patron Razumovsky, a perky theme marked by a characteristic short-short-long rhythm that dominates the movement, stated by the cello with the first violin trilling cheerfully along and duly marked "Thème Russe" in the score. Beethoven found the theme, listed as a solder's song, in a collection of Russian folk tunes.[5] While it's charming to hear the master working in a Russian idiom, it's also an unusual field of play for the very German, process-oriented Beethoven, who does indeed put the chirpy little theme through its sonata-form paces. The second theme presents a melodic profile similar to the first, but rendered smoothly rather than in the bouncy rhythm and detached notes of the opening, and accompanied by a steady hammering figure in sixteenth notes played here by the first violin. The closing theme is set in an unusual sharp, tricky rhythm, with the first violin part exceptionally high, even a bit shrill. Beethoven exploits the accompanying figure of the second theme for the first part of the development, then runs the tricky closing figure even higher, into the stratosphere. But he brings back the first theme quite elegantly and in the coda focuses more and more on the pervasive rhythm of the opening theme, slowing down once for a lyrical reflection before a final short-short-long bounce to the end.

The second of the "Razumovsky" Quartets, in E minor, runs about thirty-five or thirty-six minutes, several minutes shorter than its epic predecessor but still much longer than any string quartet by Haydn or Mozart. The tone of this great work—lyrical, tragic, passionate—is much different from the kaleidoscopic moods of Op. 59 No. 1. With the exception of the long, glowing slow movement, this work is dark in mood and much more laconic in its expressive postures and means than the F Major Quartet, or for that matter the C Major work that rounds out the opus.

The E Minor Quartet opens with a brusque gesture of two big chords, E minor and B major, stated loudly and firmly by the full ensemble. Or is it? Another, more careful listening reveals an ambiguous tone to the sequence, which Beethoven achieves by scoring the second chord with its weakest tone (D-sharp) in the bottom position, played by the cello. Instead of a stern, minor-to-minor chord sequence, Beethoven goes from minor to major, which sounds wistful, eloquent, and open-ended. The composer makes considerable use of the questioning two-chord gesture over the course of the entire movement, chords that are sometimes compared to the two crunching E-flat major chords that open the "Eroica" Symphony. There's some resemblance in the way they demand the listener's attention and perhaps even act as a call to arms, but the assertive tone of those is not matched here, and the only quality the two movements have in common is their drama. It may make just as much sense to refer to Haydn, who used chord sequences as brilliant calls to attention, as at the start of his great String Quartet, Op. 76 No. 1, which opens with a bright three-chord gesture. Mozart, too, begins countless instrumental works with gestural flourishes.

There's a long pause, after which the twisting first theme appears, following in the uneasy tone of the opening chords. After another long silence it's then repeated in F major, an unusual key for a work in E minor. This key relationship is known as a Neapolitan second; its effect on the ears and nerves of listeners will vary based on context, but here Beethoven uses it with so little preparation that it's mysterious, raising tension. After yet another silence, the theme reappears in another key, which Beethoven at last extends with a graceful but melancholy tail of sixteenth notes that lead, circularly, back to the opening chords. All this intensely focused activity has occupied about half a minute. Now more open conflict breaks out as the first violin screams out over stabbing accents from the ensemble below. This too ends soon, ushering in a more lilting theme marked by trills for the first violin over a spinning accompaniment for the middle strings. This melody lasts for just a few seconds, with a violent, chattering figure taking over and leading into the closing group, which consists of two parts: murmuring syncopated chords for the full ensemble and some furious scrambling for the ensemble highlighted by a vigorous, plummeting arpeggio for the first violin. As you've noticed, there's a lot to hear in this exposition, which often sounds spare but is in fact tightly packed. Fortunately, the composer differentiates clearly among the rhythmic profiles of the various thematic elements, from the opening theme and its kin, sometimes flowing, sometimes pause-laden, to the more angular attacks of subsequent phrases, such as the chattering theme or the angry closing part.

The development discusses all the thematic characters we've met, beginning with the pair of chords, played softly a couple of times before being spat out loudly; this is followed by the most extended iteration yet of the sinuous opening theme and the murmuring idea from the closing group. Then comes a real developmental battle in which the two-chord motto roars out, first under and then over the opening idea, rendered in a storm of falling sixteenth notes; this ends in a magnificent unison passage, begun by the cello but soon joined by all the strings. A sequence of falling trills, stated powerfully by the full quartet, leads to the recapitulation. Beethoven opens the coda as he did the development, with the two-chord motto chewed over thoughtfully a few times in shifting harmonies building to a massive, dissonant chord that paradoxically brings stasis and climax to this swiftly flowing music; an impassioned version of the opening theme leads to a tight and gloomy closing phrase.

The second movement provides the sole moment of tranquility—lots of them, actually, since it's about twelve minutes long—in this otherwise troubled work. The primary melody on which this beautiful and reflective sonata-form movement is based is in long-drawn tones for the full ensemble. The second theme, which enters over a rhythmic figure of detached notes, shows how Beethoven alters the movement's richly homogeneous sound with occasional changes in texture. The tempo never budges, and the harmony remains fairly static as well. The closing theme, a winding melody over a pulsating accompaniment, is the most tranquil of all; it is also curiously reminiscent of the first movement's restless first theme. The composer exploits the accompaniment in the development, turning it into an all-encompassing murmuring. A big outburst of long-held chords toward the end provides the only hint of disturbance in this otherwise placid passage, and the movement winds down slowly in reminiscences of the closing theme.

The scherzo that follows, in an unusual expanded ABABA form, is fantastical and unforgettable. The opening theme is a hopping tune for the violin over an unstable accompaniment that's both delicate and distinctive. Beethoven introduces a Russian theme (again, with each instrumental entry marked) into the repeated trio sections. This one, "Glory Be to God in Heaven," will be familiar to anyone who has heard Mussorgsky's opera *Boris Godunov*, where the Russian master deploys it to a very different effect in the grand coronation scene. There, accompanied by a full orchestra and belted out by the chorus, it's overwhelming; Beethoven's use is light, playful, and contrapuntally inflected. In the finale a great fiddly theme is set over a thumping dance beat, veering wildly between E minor and C major. Its thematic DNA also anticipates Beethoven's greatest quartet finale (Op. 131), though this quartet doesn't quite possess the later work's sophistication or power. But this one is enjoyable enough in its rough, middle-period way, and first-time hearers are sure to like it. The second theme is arch-shaped and more lyrical, but the pounding rhythmic pattern carries the day as a fine, quietly muttered cadence leads into the stormy coda, at a faster tempo and emphatically in E Minor. Except in the second movement, Beethoven's widely varied ways of expressing instability are the keys to grasping this enjoyable quartet.

The third and last quartet of Op. 59, in C major, is another work that's wildly unstable, too, but not in the moody manner of the E Minor Quartet. Rather, each of the four movements of this most classically styled of the set presents a radically different affect. The first movement has a dualistic nature: Beethoven follows a Mozartean model by opening with a slow, mysterious introduction leading into a bright allegro in the master's most sun-drenched style. The second movement is another singular creation, with no comparable movements by Beethoven and few by anyone else, but its melancholy posture, folklike quality, and consistency of sound set it apart definitively. The third movement is one of Beethoven's last menuettos, bland in the outer sections but with a big-shouldered, rustic trio set in as its centerpiece. And the finale is a wild, fast fugato. Supposedly the first players and audiences found this quartet a relief in comparison to its longer companions in F major and

E minor; though the shortest of the three at about thirty-two minutes, it, too, fairly overflows with eccentricities and difficulties of its own.

Discussions of the C Major Quartet always refer to Mozart's C Major Quartet, K. 465, tellingly nicknamed the "Dissonance," which begins with a slow introduction of remarkable boldness. Mozart's wandering lines for the four instruments would seem to have little in common with the slowly shifting chords in blocked out harmony here, but as one commentator points out,[6] Beethoven owes just as much to the great opening passage, "Representation of Chaos," from Haydn's oratorio *The Creation*, which is closer to Beethoven's quartet musically. Certainly all three introductions are impressive and effective in their own ways. Beethoven's is simply a sequence of unresolved chords: rather than the usual dissonance-resolution pattern we're used to, he moves from dissonance to dissonance, with a few trills attempting to bridge the unbridgeable and the cello pursuing a descending line, seemingly on its own. Finally, there seems to be a vague progress toward something, though of course first-time hearers will find it hard to guess what, just as they did in 1806. The first theme of the sonata movement that follows is a cheerful, almost offhand utterance in a springing rhythm, opened by two quiet but firmly stated notes, which leads to a radiant theme dominated by a short-short-long-long rhythm that seems to flood the scene with daylight. The cello line, deep below, bounces charmingly between its lowest note, C, and the C an octave above. The second theme, based on a rising C major scale, is a relaxed tune for the violins, echoed by the cello in its alto register. The ensemble discusses this idea at some length but then continues on its brisk, amiable way. The closing theme starts with some bustling for the cello, which then passes it to the other instruments.

Beethoven begins the inventive development with the springing figure that opened the main body of the movement, turning it into an amusingly monotonous pattern for the cello that may remind you of the winding of an old clock. He later turns the first two rising notes of the first theme into a characteristic motto, traded in a more earnest debate between the paired upper and lower instruments. A long trill and a cadenza-like phrase for the first violin lead elegantly to the

recapitulation; then the two-note motto is subjected to more exploration. And just when everything seems to be calming down, Beethoven
unexpectedly speeds up into a fiery closing phrase.

The slow movement is another one-off that would have been included
on the CD had space allowed. It's an extraordinary, very beautiful character piece that's tough to classify. Some droning harmonic effects give
it a folklike character that some hear as an impressionistic gesture by the
composer toward Russianness for the sake of Count Razumovsky, but
the piece apparently contains no specific references to Russian music.
Robert Schumann marks a passage in the first movement of his Fantasy
in C Major, Op. 17, for piano (a musical tribute to Beethoven, by the
way), to be played "in the tone of a legend," which this wonderful music
may share. The main idea is a long, lilting, melancholy tune in A minor
stated by the first violin over plucked notes by the cello, which dominate that instrument's role over the course of the movement. The long
opening melody ends in a sensitive figure in hovering sixteenth notes for
all instruments but the cello, which holds to its steady path far below.
This is succeeded by a wailing variant in F minor with an exotic quality
and a rising second theme in a more easygoing tone. The easy, rocking
rhythm holds through the length of this nine-minute movement, an
unusual strategy for the usually restless Beethoven, but one that adds
to its hypnotic effect, as do the frequent and long pizzicato passages for
the cello. And the last page of the score, with its condensed repeat of
the sensitive and wailing phrases and long, dying fall, is magical.

Beethoven looked back fondly at eighteenth-century musical manners in a number of important works. These contain minuets or ironically distant versions of them, such as the rather generic main theme of
this movement. The fine two-part trio, however, has a much stronger,
rustic profile, with a firm theme in a bounding rhythm. The composer
adds a pensive coda that also prepares the way for the breakneck finale.
This bravura movement moves at a staggering pace that is clearly
intended to challenge the performers. A strong and exciting theme for
viola opens the movement, which actually consists of several fugal passages bound with non-contrapuntal material. Later, for example, what
begins like a double fugue (one with two subjects) starts promisingly,

but the composer lets it go for the sake of the racy music of great élan that's more athletic than intellectual. At some moments it sounds almost like an overture by Rossini—hardly a bad thing, but subversive to serious contrapuntal ambitions. Yet its buoyant mood and glossy tonal surfaces provide a satisfying burst of energy to end this singular and brilliant quartet.

The "Harp" and "Serioso" Quartets, Op. 74 and Op. 95

Two works of enormous significance—the E-flat Major, Op. 74, nicknamed the "Harp," and the F Minor, aptly called by the composer "Serioso"—round out the string quartets of Beethoven's middle period. Products of 1809 and 1810 respectively, they display opposing aspects of Beethoven's art, the first spacious and lyrical, and the second tragic—one of the master's most remarkable compositions in any category—a tragic essay in ferocious compression. The gap in the opus numbers for two works that were written close together chronologically can be attributed to Beethoven's withholding publication of the F Minor Quartet until 1816. A French invasion of Vienna in 1809 made for a very unpleasant period in that city—a bombardment seems to have hastened Haydn's decline and death[1]—but Beethoven's music of this era tends toward the untroubled, or at least is immune to the expression of misery. Other works of the year include the grandiose and serene "Emperor" Piano Concerto and the piano sonata nicknamed "Les Adieux," which blends expressions of longing and joy. Both, like the Op. 74 Quartet, are in E-flat major, forming a cluster of compositions in which the composer thought consistently in that key; the Piano Trio, Op. 70 No. 2, of 1808 (see pp. 60–64) also belongs to this group.

It's easy to describe the Op. 74 as conservative when comparing it to the uncompromising "Serioso," and it has also been posited that the work was a tribute to Haydn, by which critics imply that it's in a more traditional vein. But Op. 74 was considered difficult and daring when it was first published,[2] and while it may appear mild next to its fierce successor, almost anything would; not to mention that Haydn remained a bold and unconventional composer to the end of his career. The

surprisingly common misperception of Haydn as a musical conservative stems partly from our seeing him through the lens of Beethoven's
more violent radicalism. There's certainly nothing comfortable or old-
fashioned about the E-flat Major Quartet that closes Haydn's Op. 76,
of 1797, sometimes cited as Beethoven's inspiration for Op. 74. Any
tribute by Beethoven to Haydn would surely honor the advanced aspects
of the older master's style; in any case, Beethoven's Op. 74 is better
approached on its own terms with the full consideration we'd accord
to any work of his maturity.

The E-flat Major Quartet opens with a slow introduction that's suave
but dense, an exercise in ambiguity. The very first bar, for example,
contains a note that makes the music sound as though it's in A-flat major
rather than the nominal E-flat major; and the questioning affect that
note contributes to the passage is unmistakable. Some lovely, supple
phrases follow, interrupted occasionally by big chords for all four instruments, but then Beethoven embarks on a mysterious rising sequence
in a cloudy harmony that makes the listener wonder again where he is
going. We learn soon enough that he's leading, albeit rather indirectly
from a harmonic point of view, into the first theme of the sonata-allegro
movement. But as you listen, take a moment to consider the genuine
strangeness of the introduction, in which by means of tempo and texture the composer binds together four ideas that are diverse in their
melodic, harmonic, and rhythmic patterns.

The first theme starts crisply but not too forcefully with a broken
E-flat major chord stated by the full ensemble, followed by an easygoing melody for the violin over an ambling accompaniment that blends
smoothly into a marvelous plucked second phrase accompanied by
chortling eighth notes. Beethoven's generous use of the pizzicato sound
throughout the first movement is what earned this quartet its nickname: to early listeners, the plucked strings suggested the sonority of
the harp. The next thematic element in this playful group consists of
long-held chords played in *crescendo*—increasing loudness—alternating with falling, sharply accented ones that sound rather like a sneeze
rendered musically. A bustling sequence leads to the second theme, in
long arching lines and with swiftly flowing sixteenth-note accompaniment. The excellent closing theme consists of drumming eighth notes in

a satisfying cadential phrase. The development section pits the opening violin melody against a rhythmic figure that recalls the final phrases of the introduction and rising scales, again in striking pizzicato, over the course of which the composer continually shifts his rhythmic presentation of the material.

The very long recapitulation contains many notable additions to and reinterpretations of the material, including the brisk closing theme preparing the way for a faraway sequence of long-held thoughtful chords, kin to those in the first movement of the first "Razumovsky" Quartet, though not as strange. The most beautiful passage features cadenza-like scales and arpeggios for the first violin decorating the easygoing tune that opened the allegro, here broken into fragments that are ardently stated by the rest of the ensemble in both plucked and full-throated bowed phrases.

The slow movement is a lyrical rondo in a slow tempo on complementary themes, with the main theme decorated more lavishly on each reprise. That fervent melody is sung by the first violin in a high register over a richly scored accompaniment from the rest of the ensemble. The first episode is a more delicate tune with a somewhat haunted affect. Rocking triplets animate while they decorate the second appearance of the rondo theme, and the second episode features an expressive melody shared by the first violin and cello, with the middle strings providing a flowing accompaniment. Beethoven ends this in a hesitating unison phrase that summons the haunted feeling of the first episode, making that feeling palpable and a bit menacing. In its final and most gorgeous appearance the composer decorates the rondo theme with flowing passagework and plucked notes. And the closing passage, with its detached chords that sound like gentle breathing, ends the movement in a peaceful mood.

First-time listeners will respond immediately to the energy of the memorable scherzo. Moreover, the main theme, with three short notes followed by a long one, bears a close resemblance to the famous opening of the Symphony No. 5, which Beethoven had composed in 1808. It's a great example of a Beethovenian motto-theme, a tiny idea that the composer carries much further than seems possible—and it's even in C minor, like the symphony. This four-note idea saturates almost every bar of the scherzo, though the composer treats the idea more lightly here. The trio is a burly contrapuntal passage in which high spirits and a parodistic mood are clear: its speed, faster than that of the main part of the scherzo, and its loud volume from start to finish offer anything but the normal sense of calm contrast typical of a trio; the brutal sawing Beethoven asks of the instruments is funny, while the rough counterpoint sounds like a satire of a music student's exercise. Formally, the scherzo portion appears three times, and the trio twice. The third and last appearance of the scherzo is at a soft dynamic level, which Beethoven reduces continually as the passage progresses. He leads the running passagework down a new harmonic channel, and at last we understand that the way has been prepared for the fourth movement.

The finale, six quirky variations on a curious two-part theme, is one of Beethoven's most unusual efforts in the form, yet its affect is suave and genial from start to finish. The movement has been compared to the opening movement of Haydn's E-flat Major Quartet, Op. 76 No. 6, mentioned above.[3] Certainly the themes of Haydn's and Beethoven's movements resemble one another: both are built of repetitions of short phrases, and Haydn's are only four notes long, while Beethoven's are an even terser three. Each individual phrase sounds short-winded, but the theme overall is elegant and surprisingly broad, and the composer alternates lyrical incarnations with more active ones. The first variation transforms the theme into spiky eighth notes, and in the next the viola states it in triplets, backed by the rest of the ensemble in sweet, proto-Brahmsian harmony. The third variation presents the theme in vigorous, detached notes with a running accompaniment reminiscent of Bach, even though there is no real counterpoint here. Active figuration for the cello marks the fourth variation, and in the fifth the composer breaks the theme between busy sixteenth notes for the first violin and choppy chords for the other instruments. Beethoven speeds up and quiets down in the sixth variation, where the theme is altered and compressed rhythmically over the steady pulsing of the cello below, though here he has roamed far afield, making the theme much more difficult to recognize. The astonishing coda consists of three more fragmentary variants pressing breathlessly against one another; the last presents busily rushing scales and three quiet chords to end this remarkably individual work, which really seems to have little of the traditional about it—we might even call it forward-looking.

Beethoven composed the F Minor Quartet, Op. 95—one of his greatest—in 1810. Its nickname, "Serioso," offers one of the rare cases in which the composer gave the suggestive subtitle (others are for the "Pathétique" Sonata and the "Pastoral" Symphony)—which certainly suits the character of the work, if understatedly. It's serious and more— wild, furious, desperate, and more than a little strange, like so many of the most moving efforts of the master's maturity. Well aware of its uncompromising nature, Beethoven went so far as to write that it was intended "for a small circle of connoisseurs and is never to be performed in public."[4] The key of F minor was uncommon in the classical era, and is used by Beethoven in the "Appassionata" Sonata for Piano and the dungeon scene from *Fidelio*. The quartet shares with these a mood of oppressive gloom. Two string quartets by Haydn (Op. 20 No. 5 and Op. 55 No. 2) may also serve as a precedent in their use of the rare key signature and their somber passion.

But what makes the Op. 95 quartet exceptional, beyond its unusual key, is its concentration, which is without parallel in Beethoven's work and could hardly differ more from the grandeur of the Op. 59 quartets or the offbeat lyricism of Op. 74. From start to finish, the four move- ments of the "Quartetto serioso" speak different musical and affective languages from any of its predecessors. Its laconic density may anticipate some movements in the five late quartets—the second movement of Op. 130, for example (CD Track 7)—and certainly some of the jagged string writing in the scherzo previews parts of the Great Fugue. But the continual reductionism that Beethoven adheres to here is singular in his output. The first and third movements in particular show Beethoven rigorously banning any transitional material, making the shifts between ideas abrupt and jarring.

Although the quartet's four-movement format looks ordinary from the outside, it's actually as individual as the expressive nature of the composition: there's no real slow movement, and the finale is prefaced by a slow introduction and concluded by an enigmatic passage in a dif- ferent character that has puzzled performers, audiences, and critics from the beginning. This crucial quartet is so different from anything we've heard before—but so powerful—that its opening movement is included as track 6 on the accompanying CD. It is the inverse of the first movement of the F Major Quartet, Op. 59 No. 1, which precedes it on the disc; hearing the coiled fury of the selection from Op. 95 after the expansiveness of the earlier composition should prove a startling illustration of the different characters of the two works, as well as of the impressive widening of Beethoven's stylistic range that took place over the four years that separate them.

The first movement consists of emphatic musical gestures, flung out harshly, with no padding. The first theme group, based on a turn and hammered notes, is hurled out furiously at the beginning and followed by its tail of detached notes, stated with equal vehemence, all emphatically holding the F minor tonality. At 0:09 Beethoven gives the opening idea in a more questioning tone to the cello, but starting it on a G-flat. This is the first example of the Neapolitan interval that pervades the work; remote from the home key, it's always surprising to the ear, creating a sense of mystery and drama. A more lyrical though still mournful phrase follows, into which the cello interjects eloquent rising arpeggios (0:16 and 0:19). The lyrical flow of the music seems to continue with the sweet melody sung by the first violin, but note also how Beethoven undermines it with the viola's insistent repetition of the opening turn starting at 0:21 and continuing more forcefully to 0:29, when the first theme returns in all its coiled fury. At 0:32 Beethoven inserts another brief but equally dramatic Neapolitan episode, this one a rising and falling scale that starts on a G. The lyrical mood returns as the composer moves toward the second theme, which the viola and then the cello take up in earnest at 0:40. A sharply accented chord at 0:58 disturbs the smooth contour of the idea as the viola repeats the turn again and again. Another jolting scale in the remote key of A major disrupts the music. Beethoven takes up the rest of the exposition with a wan closing theme beginning at 1:09 and further obsessive reflections on the opening turn first in the middle strings, then the cello. At 1:25 another brutal scale in a distant key—this time D major—breaks in. From a harmonic perspective, F minor and D major ordinarily have little to do with each other. But throughout the first three movements of this singular work, Beethoven uses the atypical D major as a foil for the tonic key.

The short but violent development section starts at 1:46. But it's fairly typical structurally, if not in its mode of expression or brevity, of how these passages work. It begins with fragmented reiterations of the opening material. Then, at 1:56, Beethoven reintroduces the detached-note idea, the second element of the opening theme, in the first violin over another strong rhythmic figure for the rest of the ensemble below, all while moving purposefully through different keys. At 2:07 the first violin takes up a nervously shifting figure as harmonies continue to move and the turning figure reasserts itself more and more emphatically, and the opening idea returns, marking the start of the recapitulation (2:23). The eventful development has occupied only thirty-seven seconds of the movement's playing time of 4:34—very brief but providing the listener nonetheless with a sense of having traveled a considerable distance. Beethoven expands only a little in the recapitulation, as opposed to his usual liberality with this portion of a sonata-form movement; rather than amplifying his material, he is more occupied with redistributing it. Another Neapolitan scale is heard at 2:28, and the second theme returns at 2:42. The pauses at 3:12 and 3:33 that hold the spaces between the disruptive scales and the closing theme are good examples of the uncompromisingly harsh transitions that mark the movement. The coda begins at 3:52 in the same way as the development did, and following one of the most violent passages in this savage movement, the composer battles back to F minor at 4:07. Listen to the metallic rasping of the viola at 4:11 as it obsesses over the turn sixteen times, leading into the final iterations of the opening idea. The absolute lack of rhetoric of the glum closing phrase is characteristic of Beethoven's style in the latter part of his middle period and in many late works.

Using the principle of contrast, Beethoven followed this astonishing movement, marked by a forward momentum that's perhaps unrivaled in his oeuvre, with an enervated slow movement. Paradoxically, its tempo isn't genuinely slow; but it seems to hover rather than move forward. Beethoven casts it in D major, which, as mentioned above, is highly unusual for a classical-era composition in F minor. The movement opens with the cello playing a falling scale that's deliberately phrased weakly, then a long melody in a gently rocking rhythm that rises very gradually in the first violin. This ends in diminished chords that sound like sighs or perhaps even gasps. But the overall feeling of the music suggests exhaustion. The next section is a long and serious fugue, of which the viola states the subject. But this, too, has a curiously motionless quality, and the fugue's harmony gradually grows heavy with dissonant tensions. The cello resumes the descending scale that opened the movement as the other instruments hold long, chilly chords above. The fugue resumes in an eerie thematic incarnation, and then the opening comes back, rounding out the movement's structure, which comes to an open-ended pause after a final reminiscence of the limp, falling scale. The strangeness of the music of this longest movement in the quartet is anything but calming; the composer makes it just as disturbing in its way as the raging of the opening movement.

The scherzo, to which the composer gives the singular tempo and expression marking *Allegro assai vivace, ma serioso* (quick and very lively, but serious), picks up musically and emotionally where the first movement left off. Its pause-laden main subject is marked by some tricky rhythmic work for ensemble, while the edgy, bare writing for the instruments expresses a frenzy that's barely under control—this is rough stuff. In the trio, a fragmentary melody for the second violin, viola, and cello tries to rise above a steady pattern of decorative eighth notes in the first violin. And Beethoven dips again into D major, which in this context seems cooler if not exactly refreshing. Both scherzo and trio recur, the scherzo in a faster, more frantic incarnation, to end this uneasy movement that further unsettles the attentive listener's already rattled nerves.

Though relatively short, the finale packs an enormous punch, also presenting the riddle of its surprise ending. Beethoven begins the movement with a brief (seven bars), mysterious, but beautiful slow introduction in which the four instruments, all with sighing figures, vie with one another for dominance. These merge into the opening theme of the sonata-rondo, a graceful weeping theme that blends into more furious material, including shuddering sixteenth notes and a stabbing phrase for the first violin and cello. After these, the first episode is built on a melody for the second violin and viola that speaks in stark tones of woe. Strangely quiet moments also mark the progress of this intense expression of terror and grief. The last presentation of dark material consists of an imperiously hammered, recitative-like passage interrupted by ghostly pianissimo tones in the first violin.

Then, unexpectedly, comes the coda, one of Beethoven's queerest conceptions. It's a racing passage in F major, the tonic major—the harmonic opposite of the oppressive F minor that dominates the work. A rising idea for the first violin emerges quietly (again and again, Beethoven marks this passage to be played quietly) over shimmering eighth notes for the other instruments. A couple of vigorous cadences lead to a last iteration of the glistening rising figure, and the piece ends in a tone utterly out of joint with everything that has gone before. However, the violin's rising figure recalls the alarming Neapolitan intervals of the first movement, and this astonishing passage is too incongruous and muted in its dynamics to be perceived as genuinely jolly. The coda is inevitably compared to the finale of an opera buffa, and it's certainly possible that Beethoven intended it as a parody, affectionate or otherwise, on the music of Rossini, which was enormously popular at the time. There's no question that it disrupts the mood and style of a work that otherwise displays a high aesthetic unity. And it prompts the question of why the composer placed this glittering coda at the end of one of his grandest, most intensely focused, most tragic compositions. For some it simply represents Beethoven dismissing with a figurative wave of his hand the demons he conjured. Repeated listenings may make the rest of us more comfortable with its disjunctive nature and even leave us with a sense that it works, however perversely; one begins to wonder just how else Beethoven *could* have ended it. But this is a puzzle for which no critic can provide much guidance. You just have to listen, and listen again; and decide for yourself whether the coda works.

The Late Quartets
E-flat Major, Op. 127,
and A Minor, Op. 132

Beethoven wrote the first three of the five late quartets on a commission from Prince Nikolai Galitzin, a cello-playing admirer from St. Petersburg. Therefore, curiously, six of the important string quartets of Beethoven's maturity—the three of Op. 59, as well as Opp. 127, 132, and 130/133—were commissioned by Russian noblemen. Galitzin initially contacted the composer in 1822, offering to pay for one, two, or three quartets. Busy with the *Missa Solemnis*, the Ninth Symphony, and the *Diabelli Variations*, Beethoven did not get started on the Galitzin project until 1824. Although dependent on patronage for income, Beethoven always took as long as he needed to work his compositions through to his own satisfaction, so that two years of letters from the prince pressing Beethoven on his progress were met by replies essentially saying "soon."

Beethoven completed Op. 127 in early 1825. Even though the composer was by then almost completely deaf, he supervised the rehearsals for the work's premiere, by the Schuppanzigh Quartet, by watching the movements of the players' bows. This great, opulently beautiful work was not well received by its first audiences, who found it dense and musically advanced—which it was and still is. But Beethoven's music, which was known to be difficult, was also treated with unusual respect: following the suggestion of the violinist Karl Holz, Op. 127 was played twice in several public performances of 1825—on both the first *and* the second halves of the program—to allow audiences a better opportunity to get to know it.[1]

It's easy to imagine being puzzled by a brand-new work of the scale and depth of this one. With recordings that allow us to listen at leisure and pocket scores to follow, not to mention almost two centuries of hindsight, we can easily appreciate this masterwork's abundant lyricism. Like much late Beethoven, Op. 127 is conceived on a grand scale and overflows with the melting sweetness that marks the master's last phase. Lyricism dominates the late quartets, and Op. 127 is the most lyrical of the five, the first, second, and fourth movements bursting with ripe melodic material. Only the scherzo strikes a different, spikier note. Beethoven holds Op. 127 to a standard-looking four-movement format that is, however, extraordinary in the composer's treatment of the individual parts. While the first movement is in sonata form, for example, the thematic ideas complement rather than contrast with each other, and their development is more interplay than battle, highlighting their kinships. And the finale dissolves into an ecstatic closing of the kind we hear only in late Beethoven.

The first movement opens with a grand gesture of eleven huge chords for the full ensemble, an impressive but mellow passage that leads into the main section. The opening chords are significant for several reasons, though. First, they recur twice more over the course of the movement and therefore participate in its process, rather than acting merely as introductory mood setters. Beethoven also gives them the tempo designation *maestoso*—majestic—which he uses rarely, and only when he wants to make sure players give the passage the full grandeur he intends. Listen, too, for the rising scale the composer buries inside the first violin and cello lines, giving lift and momentum to a phrase that would otherwise sound static.[2] The final chord melts into a fervent trill, out of which the first theme emerges in two phrases, beginning with six steady quarter notes. These then break into four delicate falling eighth notes followed by a quarter note; this second phrase will later dominate the movement. The second part of the opening group is a brisk, Haydnesque idea that emerges over a bustling accompaniment, but as you listen, note the independence of the four instrumental lines, a new technique that Beethoven developed and that carries into all the late quartets. The real second theme, another gorgeous idea in G minor, emerges, and a closing theme of mock-stern chords and trills appears. Then Beethoven reintroduces the opening chords, this time in G major, for what we may be surprised to find is the development section, of which the tone is gentle and the movement dancelike. The texture here is a dense tapestry of motivic exchanges quietly dominated by smooth contrapuntal treatments of the lyrical first theme, with little of the thematic fragmentation typical of earlier developments. Beethoven works the big opening chords in here, too, for one last heaven-storming incarnation. Eventually the recapitulation steals in, but the form is more flexible and less given to rhetoric than anything we've heard before. Finally, the delicate eighth-note figure takes over, dominating the coda to a remarkable extent. For Beethoven, this remarkably fertile five-note motto yields an infinite number of mutations as it's passed, always gently, from high to low, instrument to instrument, and key to key. And indeed, he ends the movement with it in a soft and exquisitely phrased question.

The slow movement, a set of six and a half remarkable variations on a long, lyrical theme, is the quartet's center of gravity. Be prepared, in case you're listening for the first time: it runs for nearly fifteen minutes. It's not Beethoven's longest slow movement (that of the "Hammerklavier" Sonata for Piano takes that prize) nor his most austere (that of the Op. 132 quartet, which we'll look at next, is the winner there). But this is a movement that you must listen to receptively if you wish to absorb Beethoven's deliberate pace and gigantic structure.

The movement opens with a string sonority carefully built by the composer from the bottom up: the cello enters softly in the rocking rhythm of the theme, after which the viola, followed by the second and then the first violins, steals in, forming a rich harmony. Once the entire ensemble is in place, the theme, long-breathed and lilting, emerges in the first violin. The cello sings its second half, and an ineffably sweet closing phrase in a strongly rocking rhythm closes it out. The first variation moves in shorter notes that give the impression of a slight increase in momentum, but in fact its pulse—the speed and meter of the music—is identical to that of the theme. Beethoven does, however, darken the harmony and broaden the dynamics from the even quiet of the opening page with phrases that are both louder and softer. Beethoven speeds up the tempo a bit for the cheerful second variation as the violins entwine in a lavish descant, in which the theme is buried, over a dancing accompaniment by the viola and cello. An abrupt shift of harmony and tempo takes the third variation to a lofty meditation on the theme. Beethoven moves forcefully from the prevailing key of the movement to one that's very remote, while slowing the tempo down to an *adagio molto espressivo* (slow and very expressively), which is even slower than that of the theme. The feeling these alterations produce is one of great distance from what has gone before. The violin and cello share the presentation of the melody in long phrases reminiscent of deep breathing.

Beethoven returns to the original speed and key for the fourth variation, in which the first violin and cello again share the theme, decorating it with trills; finally, however, the middle strings—the second violin and viola—take up the theme in swelling dynamics and long tied notes in a new and powerful rhythmic profile. There's another enormous key change in the fifth variation, giving an overcast feeling to the music, and the composer returns briefly to the original rhythmic profile. In the sixth variation the violin decorates the theme in running sixteenth notes, with the rest of the ensemble stating the theme in gently halting fashion below. Then the instruments switch roles—the first violin soars above running notes by the other instruments below—and a climactic phrase in which all the instrumental voices merge sweetly ends the passage. There's a pause, and a pulsing seventh variation tries to get going, but fails, and after one last, eloquent exchange for the full ensemble, the movement ends quietly, on an unrhetorical, upward-reaching phrase.

Plucked chords that playfully recall the massive sequence that opened the work kick-start the scherzo and strike a new tone. The composer follows the little pizzicato fanfare with a theme in detached notes and a short-long rhythm that pervades the movement with its splendid but stiff motion, which finally threatens to swamp the whole structure. At this point, in a masterstroke of freedom and assurance, Beethoven shifts into a completely different tempo and time signature. The trio moves at a faster pace and in swift, slithering legato notes that contrast completely with the sharp rhythm that dominates the scherzo, and Beethoven places a big, lusty tune at its center for good measure. The composer also brings back a recollection of the trio before the final mordant bars of the scherzo.

The finale is one of Beethoven's most remarkable inspirations and constructions. The opening section is a rustic sonata-form movement that feels like a rondo. The composer follows this with a long, profound, disembodied coda that ends the work on another, higher plane. The composer achieves this dichotomy by subjecting the same material to radically different treatment in the movement's main and closing sections, but his achievement is singular: no one who listens with any care at all can miss the ascent from the earthly exposition and development to its heavenly conclusion, so vast are the transformations in tone and texture. The opening group begins with a big rising gesture, which leads into a plain spinning theme that cycles around the same five notes, which the composer presents in a thousand slightly altered incarnations before their big transformation in the coda. The feeling is reminiscent of a Haydn finale, but the texture is busier. A second, very countrified theme leads into a big, even rough climax with the feel of a German dance. Another secondary theme is introduced with delicacy, then reprised, comically, with great bluster. Suddenly, however, the time signature shifts to a more flowing 6/8, and trills and shivering runs take over as Beethoven puts the themes through rapid, deeply expressive changes of key. What was rough and rustic suddenly whispers and sighs, and the textures and dynamics create by far the lightest, most sublime treatment of the main theme yet. With a new rhythmic profile Beethoven transforms that homely spinning first theme into a bird of paradise, making it shudder with unmistakable ecstasy, capped by one last, soaring incarnation for the first violin over runs for the middle strings and a deep tremolando in the cello. Once you've heard the extraordinary conclusion to this great work, you'll have a much clearer sense of why so many adjectives of the spiritual variety get tossed at late-period Beethoven.

The Op. 127 quartet speaks a language of mind and spirit beyond our common experience, and we must make the effort to raise our perceptions to its level. The second of the "Galitzin" Quartets, the Op. 132 in A Minor, on the other hand, while every bit as advanced musically as its predecessor, seems clearly to portray a suffering that most of us can connect with. It is, in that sense, perhaps the most approachable of the big four of the last five (the Op. 135 quartet, though equally sublime, is less ambitious in form and scope). What most listeners hear in the deeply emotional Op. 132 are pain and grief of a most earthly sort, a conditional relief from that pain at its end, and a prayerful hymn of gratitude on a higher spiritual plane in the immense slow movement, the work's capstone and longest section by far. Part of our comprehension of Op. 132 stems from its biographical aspect, which the composer himself wove into its fabric, giving us an opportunity to observe through his art Beethoven's reaction to a serious illness.

Beethoven worked on the first two movements of Op. 132 in early 1825. In April of that year, he came down with apparently the most serious of the intestinal illnesses that plagued him, for he was too sick to work for a month or so. His stern physician, Dr. Anton Braunhofer, took Beethoven off coffee, wine, and spicy food. Within several weeks, Beethoven was recovering and planning the slow movement of his current quartet to be a hymn of thanks for his recovery. Beethoven's title for this vast and deeply moving section was "Sacred song of thanks from a convalescent to the Godhead, in the Lydian Mode." (The Lydian mode is an old musical scale used in church music through the sixteenth century.) Even though Beethoven wrote the first movement before he got sick, there's little question as to its raw emotion; so the human condition that most hear as the quartet's emotional subtext predated the illness, the recovery from which inspired the hymn of thanks. And the finale, composed after the spring illness, also expresses considerable sorrow. As portraits of the composer show, Beethoven was aging rapidly by this time, and even though he was only fifty-four in the spring of 1825, physical illness was taking a toll on him. But his mind and spirit miraculously remained vibrant even in his final illness, two years later. Beethoven finished the A Minor Quartet in July 1825.[3] While he keeps to a four-movement format for Op. 127, the Op. 132 is in a daring five movements. It's also the first of the three quartets with an unconventional multiplicity of movements, six in Op. 130 and seven in Op. 131. As noted in chapter 8, the out-of-sequence opus numbering stems from the fact that several publishers were involved in its potential publication; also, Op. 132 wasn't published until after Beethoven's death.

The character of this great work seems easier to describe than that of its fellows. As noted, the first and fifth movements are filled with suffering and sorrow; the composer manages to end the work with a closing passage that's happy, if only conditionally so, something like the coda of Op. 127. Beethoven prefaces the first movement with an introductory passage that's short but almost impenetrable musically, and dark in mood. The second movement is a wonderful piece in the style of a minuet, with a celestial trio; the brief fourth is a little march followed by a passionate recitative. And the third, as noted, is the mighty "convalescent's song of thanks," infinitely moving but simple in structure and straightforward in its two affects. In general, the first and last movements are anxious in mood and intimate, never thunderous, in their modes of expression. The beautiful main theme of the finale was considered by the composer for use in the last movement of the Symphony No. 9 before he settled on the idea of the choral ending.[4] Like Op. 127, the A Minor Quartet seems lyrical rather than dramatic, but clearly it expresses something quite different from the ecstasy of its predecessor. As in Op. 127, Beethoven handles contrasting thematic groups differently from before: in the first and fifth movements, for instance, where ideas seem to sprout from one another, and developmental battles among themes are kept to a minimum. Also, as Kerman has shown,[5] Beethoven masks the boundaries between the exposition, development, and recapitulation in the first movement, even fundamentally changing the ways in which these sections function. For example, in the depressed context of this movement, he turns the development, heretofore usually the peak of conflict and inventive fantasy, into the emotional low point.

The work opens with a slow eight-bar passage, about forty-five seconds in duration, but which forms a motto-theme based on the first four notes that dominates the movement, and, indeed, the entire work. It consists of a series of built-up chords, some bitingly dissonant, all somber and dark-hued. The cello begins and the viola and the two violins come in afterward in overlapping entries that are all essentially repetitions of the first four notes. The first violin plays a flourish in the allegro tempo of the body of the movement, but the cello, playing very high in its register, sings the sorrow-laden first theme in its characteristic rocking rhythm, with a long-short tail drawn from the first theme, that pervades much of the movement. A long passage in the same rhythm leads at last to a breakthrough into a major key and the gentle second theme, a great lyric inspiration that like everything here has a melancholy undertone. The singing quality of this theme is striking—a couple of hearings and you'll find yourself humming along with it. A closing theme based on the long-short rhythm attempts a show of strength but is cut off by long notes restating the introduction. The introductory material also returns, stretched into longer notes, to open the development. Here Beethoven presents the main theme over and over, but clothed in uncertain harmonies; a pause leads to a new idea, also in a rocking rhythm—there is a whole family of them here—by the lower strings. And again the opening chords burst in, this time in impressive fortissimo; all attempts by other themes to change the subject seem to end in the somber motto. The hovering harmonic treatment of the initial rocking idea continues, but then the second theme finds its way back in. An unassuming little march joins the proceedings but is quickly supplanted by the lyrical second theme. From this point, however, march elements take on a larger role in the movement's progress. Some tormented passagework leads to a reprise of the main theme; this Beethoven pairs with the gloomy motto chords, which the first violin finally sings out sorrowfully, high up and in long notes. The second theme makes a final appearance as the coda begins with the rocking first theme, presented in a sharp and fiery rhythmic incarnation over an accompaniment of stinging sixteenth notes. The dark but delicate passage that closes the movement features the motto theme over a continuation of the shuddering sixteenth notes in a stronger march rhythm, which dominates the coda; then, out of the sixteenth-note accompaniment rises a startling, stirring call to battle by the first violin. But this particular battle is over before it ever gets going.

Beethoven knew that the emotional rigors of the first movement needed to be mollified. The second movement, styled as a minuet, offers soothing sounds and affect and more: it's also a tribute to the menuetto of Mozart's A Major Quartet, K. 464, which Beethoven had long admired. (You may recall that Beethoven's own Quartet in A Major, Op. 18 No. 4, of twenty-five years earlier was also the fruit of his study of K. 464.) The resemblance is mostly restricted to the rising figure that opens both movements—and the key, of course. This suave melody in A major charms and calms after the first movement's tribulations. The second phrase, which falls in symmetrical reply, is typical of high-classical instrumental minuets, providing a comforting sense of partici-pating once again in that great tradition. But the trio takes the listener into regions found only in late Beethoven. It's nominally a little suite of German dances, a rustic species that the composer turns into something divine. It opens with a droning dance. Typically composers imitating the drone of bagpipes or country bands go for darker instrumental colors to parody the rough, rumbling sounds of the instruments they're copying. But here the violin's drone goes up: the heavenward reach of the violin's inverted drone is the transfiguration of daily experience by a creative consciousness. The dances that follow grow increasingly rough, but only in the delicately transfigured manner of the first dance—they too are disembodied, purged of all flesh, anachronistically prefiguring those climactic processions in the films of Federico Fellini where the director takes a loving roll call of his characters. Consider, too, when you hear this little suite of transfigured German dances, that it's only the middle section of one of the secondary movements in Op. 132, and not its high point. The composer rounds out the trio with the dance on the inverted drone, then repeats the full A section of this structurally straightforward (ABA) but cathartic take on the high-classical menuetto.

The highest point follows, but be prepared when you listen to give it the time—typically at least fifteen minutes—and the attention that one of Beethoven's grandest conceptions requires. The tempo of much of the "Heiliger Dankgesang"—the sacred song of thanks—as Beethoven himself called it, is mostly very slow, but its structure is simple. This expression of gratitude for a return to health by the fifty-four-year-old master at the height of his powers is profound, and profoundly moving. If its length and gravity put you off initially, don't worry; just keep trying. Sooner or later—probably sooner—its austere beauty and depth of feeling will come through.

The movement has two thematic elements: the very slow hymn of thanks, which we'll call A, appearing three times, and an alternating section, B, in a new key, a different rhythm, and a somewhat livelier tempo. The form of Beethoven's vast structure is simply ABABA, with both parts varied after their initial presentations. Beethoven wrote the hymn (the A sections) in the Lydian mode, an archaic harmonic pattern from which accidentals (the sharps and flats, or the black keys on a piano) are excluded. The result is a tonal purity that's hard to keep interesting for ears accustomed to the fuller harmonies of later music. It may remind you of music by the high Renaissance composer Palestrina. Beethoven brings it off brilliantly by making the hymn share the stage generously with the extensive B section, which he titles "Neue Kraft fühlend"—feeling new strength—and by putting each of the hymn's three appearances in a different rhythmic guise. The hymn opens in overlapping phrases that in their texture recall the motto theme that opens the work. But the atmosphere is utterly different: pain and gloom are replaced by radiant music and a high emotion that one can readily grasp. So slow is the initial movement of the hymn that the thirty measures of its first presentation take almost three and a half minutes to play. The passage moves with a deliberate slow smoothness of rhythm, completely without variation or drive.

A change in harmony and a pick-up in rhythmic momentum heralds the start of the alternating "Neue Kraft fühlend" section, in a slightly firmer tempo, a regular, modern key (D major), and a halting dance rhythm. It's full of short notes, common in late Beethoven, and while no less fervent than the opening section, it movingly expresses a more comprehensible, human side of the composer's emotion. The first violin holds the theme of the hymn in long notes in its second appearance, but the three lower parts show more movement. The music seems to revolve slowly compared to the near-stillness of the hymn's first iteration; the new rhythm also gives a new, melting sweetness to the harmony, based on the resolution of each dissonance created by the rhythmic dislocation. Rhythm and harmony are one thing; the emotion, again, seems expressed at once unfathomably yet comprehensibly. The "Neue Kraft fühlend" recurs, the composer making it reach a bit higher in its second appearance. Finally, the first eight-note phrase of the "Heiliger Dankgesang" is restated alone in a new, more fluid phrasing. Then it's subjected to intensive contrapuntal treatment in an astonishing display of compositional virtuosity, where Beethoven makes much of his limited material. The composer instructs that this final time it be played *Mit innigster Empfindung*—his beautiful direction meaning "with the most intimate sentiment." At last the thing begins to break gently apart, and one last questioning sequence leads to the closing chords, set in a high register for the whole ensemble.

Transitions from long, sublime slow movements to active finales became a specialty of the composer's by necessity. Two other late works display the wide range of his approaches to the problem. The "Hammerklavier" Sonata for Piano (1817) has the longest slow movement of all, followed by a violent, fugal finale, which Beethoven introduces by means of a long transitional passage that moves in stages from dreamy to wildly excited. In the case of the Ninth Symphony (1824), the composer bridges the gap to the choral finale with a long and complex passage for orchestra, eventually joined by the voice of the bass solo singer in which snatches from the first three movements are floated, then "rejected" by orchestral interjections before the bass enters with a solo dismissing what has passed and preparing the way aesthetically and aurally for the rest of the soloists and chorus with the entry of the human voice. Obviously there are no singers in the A Minor Quartet, but there are some resemblances between the case of the Ninth and the way the master achieves this difficult transition in Op. 132.

Beethoven's procedure in this quartet is probably the most straightforward of the three. He writes a two-minute movement with two parts, the first a spunky little march that rather incongruously follows the celestial close of the "Heiliger Dankgesang," followed by a darker, operatically inspired passage that copies the style of a passionate recitative to set the mood for the finale. The trim march that occupies the first half of this two-part movement inevitably startles the listener a bit after the end of the sublime slow movement, as almost anything would. It has the effect of bringing one back to earth but is mild-mannered enough not to shock. Suddenly some running notes signal change, and indeed, the first violin launches into its emotional, even slightly coarse mock recitative over tremolandi by the rest of the ensemble. In fact, it's quite reminiscent of the well-known bass solo in the finale of the Ninth ("O Freunde, nicht diese Töne . . ."), though less bluff and cheerful and, because it is a parody, much stranger. It repeats, slows down, speeds up, then slows down again as the composer leads us with a sense of harmonic and affective inevitability to the finale.

Even on first hearing, this rondo with a development section should make complete sense. It's based on a fine-boned waltz theme that's one of the master's most beautiful, and that works its way into your mind immediately, at least in part by means of its many repetitions. The surging three-note phrase, which reaches higher on each of its three repetitions, is passionate and deeply moving—Beethoven's marking for the movement is *allegro appassionato*. The mood of this sonata-rondo looks back to the pain of the first movement, which it balances and completes. Here a distinct edge of regret seems to be laid over the sorrow. The episodes generally act as complements to the glorious main theme; one peculiar exception to listen for is a mysterious fugato begun by the cello and viola, taken up by the violins. This leads into an increased tempo and a shrill reiteration of the waltz. But, in an unexpected paradox, out of this pain-laced phrase sprouts the consolatory closing passage, which you'll notice right away by the switch to A major, the brighter harmonic sibling of the prevailing A minor—it sounds as though the sun has come out. From the more delicate textures Beethoven imposes on this long and crucial coda, another heartfelt, highly memorable tune emerges, as does the sturdy phrase that closes the work. What's expressed here, so different from the thundering triumph of an Op. 59 coda, is a victory that's hard-won and far from certain.

The Mad Divertimento

The Quartet in B-flat Major, Op. 130, and the Great Fugue, Op. 133

Beethoven worked on the third and last of the quartets commissioned by Prince Nikolai Galitzin in the second half of 1825. As noted earlier, the Quartet in B-flat Major has two alternative endings: the massive *Grosse Fuge*—the Great Fugue—which was separated from the work by the composer and published separately as Op. 133; and the shorter, lighter finale Beethoven wrote in late 1826 as its replacement, the composer's last completed work. In live performances today, the Great Fugue is usually played as the finale, then typically the replacement of 1826 as a mandatory encore. Recorded versions of Op. 130 almost always contain both endings, enabling listeners to try one or the other at their pleasure.

The dual ending is only the greatest of the difficulties surrounding Op. 130, without question the most problematic of the quartets and perhaps the most difficult work in the Beethoven canon. What makes it so difficult, in addition to the two very different endings, is its apparent lack of the kinds of thematic or affective unity that so strongly mark the other late quartets—but not only the late quartets. The Op. 130 seems to stand alone in Beethoven's serious work in the diversity of its six (or seven) movements. Some listeners perceive in it a family resemblance with the suite or the divertimento—as the name suggests, a musical diversion of a light nature, often background music to parties in the palaces of the eighteenth-century aristocracy. Yet, as you'd expect, many of the divertimenti by Mozart, the greatest practitioner of the multimovement divertimento, demand one's attention with their quality and high polish. Perhaps the Op. 130 quartet bears a kinship with that genre.

Overloaded with five wildly diverse movements followed by either a fifteen-minute contrapuntal apocalypse or the tamer but still magnificent second finale, the B-flat Major Quartet can sound like a mad divertimento in which the deaf and isolated Beethoven aimed the heavy artillery of his late style at a mixed bag of musical forms, from the pretty but neutral German dance originally written for Op. 132 that became its fourth movement to the fugue, then strung them together, not quite randomly. Perhaps an obvious unity wasn't Beethoven's goal here; but if you've never heard either Op. 130 or Op. 133, be prepared for the disjunctive nature of the movements of which it is comprised, and always keep an open mind about its perceived weaknesses. Make no mistake: this ungainly vessel holds much great music. I have found that my mood on a given day will make me hear it as less or more cohesive, as will different performances, with some being more convincing about its ultimate unity.

Many of Beethoven's sketches for Opp. 130 and 133 have survived. Barry Cooper, one of Beethoven's best modern biographers, has summarized them in a way that suggests this was a work for which the composer's path was uncommonly difficult:

> Beethoven's sketches reveal that when he completed these two movements [the first and second] he had very little idea what would follow. The key and nature of the third movement had not been fixed, although it would have to be some kind of slow movement; nothing concrete had been decided about the finale; and it was also unclear how many movements there would be altogether.[1]

As noted, the fourth movement had already been written and passed over for Op. 132; Beethoven only had to transpose its key to make it fit here. And how a fugue—especially this mammoth—became the finale seems equally baffling. Beethoven had come up with the fugue's basic idea as a possible finale for the Op. 127 quartet. A keeper of sketches who valued all ideas, old and new, Beethoven apparently began developing the idea over the year between his work on the E-flat Major Quartet and the Great Fugue. As Cooper also points out, Beethoven's study of counterpoint generally, and of the music of Bach specifically, had long been a major inspiration.[2] Beethoven's completion of the quartet was delayed by months as he worked on the massive fugue.

The inner workings that allowed Beethoven to abandon the Great Fugue as the finale of the quartet are another mystery. Although initially defensive about keeping its place in the quartet, he was ultimately persuaded by Matthias Artaria, its publisher, and his friend the violinist Karl Holz that the fugue finale was more than players could perform and audiences could grasp. In any case, it's unusual that the stubborn and ambitious composer agreed. The need for the extra money he earned from the separate publication of the fugue, while perhaps not entirely discountable, seems out of character for Beethoven, for whom artistic considerations were paramount. Perhaps he had simply come to the same conclusion himself: "he may have decided that the Quartet required a catharsis, a return to normality, an epilogue in full daylight, a simple descent to earth, a reversion to classicism such as we find in the new finale."[3]

Beethoven's own generation and one or two that followed found all the late quartets too complex and difficult; in these decades they were rarely played and little understood. But by the late nineteenth century their measure had been taken: Richard Wagner, for example, was an admirer of and advocate for Op. 131. In the twentieth, some, including Schoenberg, argued for the restoration of the Great Fugue as the finale of Op. 130. And that is where taste presently stands in musical circles, of which the chamber music community is one of the most earnest segments. While some claim to hear in the fugue the culmination of the first five movements, for others it comes out of nowhere and overwhelms the rest. For some, the fugue seems unquestionably like too much and the replacement, uncomfortably, like too little. The composer's own ambivalence shows that there really is no right or wrong answer as to which finale works better. Kerman, who wonders whether the structural triumphs of the last two quartets (Opp. 131 and 135) did not cast the B-flat Major and its problems into a new light for the master, surmises:

> In short, I am inclined to take Beethoven's replacement of the Fugue as an acknowledgment . . . that he saw something wrong with the way it sat in the quartet. But I also take it that the problem could not be met at all so simply. It ran much deeper than the finale. . . . He proposed a sunny, gay, classicizing, Haydnesque conclusion; and that, too, obviously, provided no true solution.[4]

And of course, time to recast Op. 130 ran out for Beethoven, whose final illness came on shortly after he completed the replacement finale. He wasn't planning to die in March 1827, and it's possible that had he lived longer he might have returned to work on the B-flat Major Quartet once again.

The brilliant first movement looks back a bit in its clear-cut sonata structure, and in the diversity and individual character of its themes, but Beethoven's treatment of his material is volatile and often strange. The movement opens with a slow introductory passage that's grave but mellow. As in Opp. 127 and 132, Beethoven brings it back several times over the course of the movement, but this passage, being longer and more developed, is also more disruptive in its later appearances. The first theme of the main part is notable for its stabbing long-long-short-short-long rhythm, which emerges over busy descending figuration by the first violin. But a truncated and compressed version of the opening passage interrupts almost as soon as the first theme has been stated. Again the stabbing theme starts up, finally making its full statement, trailed by a busy and fantastical second part. Turns for the cello introduce the second theme, an arch-shaped lyrical tune, followed by a memorable second phrase, notable for its grumbly but charming rhythmic incisiveness. A big closing group featuring thematic fragments all bound together by the descending sixteenth-note figuration that decorated the stabbing theme is followed by a whispered four-note phrase. For the first time since the Op. 74 quartet of 1809, the composer calls for a full repeat of the exposition, including the slow introduction.

The development section is one of the master's strangest passages, but it contains many beauties nonetheless. First there's a back-and-forth between the short phrases in the two tempos—those of the slow opening and the allegro theme. Then, over an accompaniment in a limping long-short rhythm, Beethoven passes a soaring phrase based on the second theme, stated in a new rhythm between the cello and the first violin. The stabbing motif finds its way in, too. The harmonic changes here are strange, giving the passage a deeply inward, meditative affect. Soon the rushing sixteenth notes reenter, and the recapitulation is under way. Its wayward harmonic structure is colored by the mood of the development, and Beethoven ends the movement wittily on an emphatic cadence in the condensed essence (short-short-long) of the stabbing theme.

The almost continual surprises of the opening movement are followed by a different kind of shock: a muttering, highly compressed, two-minute scherzo built on two ideas (CD Track 7). This nervous and hectic little passage in B-flat minor—the relative minor of the key of the quartet—flies along at an almost shocking speed, obsessively repeating its few phrases. The opening phrase, repeated immediately, is matched by a mirror image starting at 0:12 that's also repeated. The middle section, in a new time signature, scrambles along with two repeats of its own, from 0:24 until 1:11, when a sequence of slower notes interspersed with falling scales brings back the opening phrase at 1:24. Listen for the trills and pizzicato notes that Beethoven throws toward the end in to season the material.

What's surprising about this tiny movement is its relative simplicity, even though nothing Beethoven wrote in 1825 can fairly be called simple. Musically it's pretty straightforward, from its unadorned ABA form to the folklike character of the themes and its amusing ill temper. Like many commentators, Kerman finds a resemblance to some of the late Bagatelles for Piano (Opp. 119 and 126), which are similarly short and angular.[5] What's harder to understand is its place following the opening movement's ambitions. And the third movement, while far more spacious, seems difficult to fit in, too (CD Track 8; these two sequential movements have been included to show the range of styles the composer squeezed into the quartet).

In a moderate tempo and relaxed mood, the andante that follows contrasts wonderfully with the scherzo, and with the first movement, for that matter. Where the scherzo is stripped down and breathless, this is gracious and remarkable for the care Beethoven exercised in elaborating the instrumental parts. Unlike the first movement, it's consistent from start to finish in its relaxed, playful, elegant affect. After an opening sigh in B-flat minor—the key of the scherzo, easing the transition between the movements—the music moves to D-flat major. Over a chugging accompaniment by the cello, a very gracious tune enters at 0:12. A companion, every bit as charming, enters at 0:45. A strong accent at 1:11 fails to disturb the flow of the ideas, carried along on one of the most richly wrought backgrounds Beethoven ever devised: there's really nothing else by him quite like it. What passes for a big climax in this easygoing atmosphere comes at 1:47, but it, too, is smooth and untroubled. A pizzicato phrase at 3:08 leads to a passage in which Beethoven breaks the theme into mincing repeated notes in a rocking rhythm. Another delicious flourish comes at 3:54, when the cello takes up a grunting grace note as part of its contribution. A trill at 4:34 leads to a varied restatement of the opening theme, and a cool new harmony enters at 5:41, signaling the start of the coda. Note the instruments' shuddering at 6:11, right before the closing cadence.

This rich and active movement is fun to follow with a printed score. Another reason to follow along in the score is to get a sense of the manic energy Beethoven put into the movement. What sounds easygoing and spontaneous may startle you when you see it in print and consider the nervous system that created it—and realize the degree of artifice required to make it sound so relaxed.

This elegant movement represents a peak of Beethoven's sophistication. But having gotten to know the powerful unities of the Op. 127 and Op. 132 quartets that are this quartet's companions, let alone the C-sharp Minor that will follow, the question arises, again: leaving aside Beethoven's little connection by means of key between the second and third movements, what do these discrete musical movements have to do with each other? What unifies them?

The fourth movement does little to answer that question. This straightforward waltz, as noted above, was intended for Op. 132 but did not fit into the tight structure that evolved for that work. And so it wound up here. Its title, Alla danza Tedesca, means "in the manner of a German dance." And its ABA form resembles that of the second-movement scherzo, but the affect here is conventionally gracious. To maintain musical interest at this lower emotional pitch, Beethoven makes the phrases uneven and uses some canonic imitation to enliven the trio. The main melody is varied charmingly in the reprise, with the melody carried in smoothly flowing notes over some more rustic bumping by the rest of the quartet. And finally, in a more startling idea, Beethoven breaks the tune up among the ensemble, with each instrument playing alone and the rest remaining silent as they pass the theme around.

The composer follows this most neutral movement in the quartet with the most emotionally laden, the beautiful Cavatina. Beethoven adopted the name from opera, where it describes the lyrical section of the standard two-part aria known as the cavatina-cabaletta. The first violin sings a fervent, hymnlike melody over an accompaniment by the rest of the ensemble that's far more than mere harmonic background, with every instrument making its own vibrant contribution to the movement's lyric unity. The tune itself will likely stick in your head after a few hearings, and you can expect it to haunt you afterward. Out of nowhere, the lower instruments shift gears into throbbing triplets in a heavy new harmony. The first violin reenters in broken phrases in an astonishing imitation of vocal style, which Beethoven famously marks *beklemmt*—oppressed or suffocated. What we hear in this passage is a profound, choking grief, expressed with the highest artistry. The mood gently lifts as the cavatina section returns, its beauty rendered far more poignant by its contrast with the darkness of the central section. Some find in this wonderful movement the thread that finally pulls—or starts to pull—the Op. 130 quartet together, while for others it's yet another disparate, albeit profound page.

Whatever you come to believe about the appropriateness of the new finale for Op. 130, there's no denying its brilliance. Beethoven cleverly designed the movement to sound like an old-fashioned rondo, but in fact it's in a highly sophisticated sonata form. At nine minutes' playing time, this is also a substantial movement, and no lightweight, despite its prevailingly bright tone. Beethoven starts the movement by copying a trick of Haydn's: opening on a hopping rhythmic figure given to the viola in a harmony other than the B-flat major in which the movement is cast. As you listen, you'll note the way the theme's entry seems to pull the harmony up to the "correct" key. And the mock-rustic theme itself, though fine-boned, is so delicious that it should lodge in your memory in no time. The fluid second theme provides more traditionally lyrical contrast to what is essentially a lyric conception. Everything moves quickly in this richly detailed and rhythmically incisive movement, where only two climactic moments briefly interrupt the witty flow. Also, in his typical manner, Beethoven finds room for a few reflective moments.

The interest here never flags, thanks to the composer's enrichment of his material, which he constantly redistributes across the ensemble, adding new comments by the other instruments; brief, delicate shifts of harmony throw the themes into different lights, and of course he uses astonishingly varied ways of presenting thematic material, from apparently straightforward to busily contrapuntal. For example, toward the end of the development, after a long, polished fugato passage, Beethoven thunders out the theme with unexpected force, while in the recapitulation he builds the dance rhythm of the theme into a brief but ecstatic climax. After this, the quartet, led by the first violin, takes up a noble "fiddling" variant of the theme, where, in the manner of Haydn, the melody is woven into a steady flow of sixteenth notes as the rest of the ensemble presses on with its powerful rhythm.

This lovable movement stands brilliantly on its own, so don't feel guilty about enjoying it that way. And it's touching that Beethoven's last completed piece is a tribute to both his teacher Haydn and to the high-classical style to which he himself kept returning, but which he also stretched to the point of destruction.

The Great Fugue, Op. 133

The German title for the original finale of the B-flat Major Quartet is *Grosse Fuge,* which in the French translation, *Grande fugue,* seems most resonant, descriptive, and reverent. To that French translation, given on the first page of the score, the composer also added the curious subtitle *tantôt libre, tantôt recherchée*—somewhat free, somewhat studied. Beethoven's remarkable little description of his contrapuntal methods in this immense movement may serve to help both new listeners and those who've heard the work and found it tough going. Nothing will ever make easy listening of this most advanced—"contemporary forever," in Stravinsky's immortal critique—of Beethoven's works; the composer didn't want it that way. But if you break it into its component sections and realize that the composer balances the fugal, "studied" parts carefully with freer, nonfugal passages that are a bit less aggressive in tone, the piece becomes somewhat more approachable, though it will never be a cakewalk. Even though Beethoven was uncompromising, remember that he was a master of variation and pacing who knew that his great essay in contrapuntal thought could not remain in a uniformly harsh tone from start to finish.

If you've never heard the Great Fugue, you need to prepare yourself for a hard ride; if you've tried to listen to it and found just it too difficult or unpleasant, you have plenty of company. But anyone who undertakes the project needs to accept the music's long uncushioned stretches, which Beethoven meant to sound rugged and imposing. His goal was not to write a pretty piece, but to compose an Everest of an essay in a new contrapuntal manner, paying tribute to Bach and Handel while displaying his own mastery of a new style. Beethoven's other fugue resembling this one in scope and ferocity is the finale of the "Hammerklavier" Sonata for Piano, Op. 106. Beethoven didn't mean to please audiences with movements like these; rather, he intended that they be heard in awe, and surely the best way to approach the work is with respect. With or without you and me, the Great Fugue will endure.

The Great Fugue is divided into five broad sections, played without a break, which scholars further subdivide into ten.[6] Beethoven calls the short but stunning opening passage the Overtura. This is followed by the first fugue, a long, rough passage. The second fugue, third of the five broad sections, is in fact a blend of fuguelike and other materials and is more mellow in tone. A brisk, marchlike transition leads into the third and most formidable fugue—the fourth big section—which is even more thorny than the first. The march returns to lead the way into the fifth and last part, a huge and powerful closing. The five big divisions are fairly clear, but the chart below may help you find your way through. The timings are based on the performance by the Kodály Quartet on the same Naxos label recording used on the CD in the back of the book, which comes in at 15:59 overall. The three other performances of the fugue I have at hand are all close in timing, from 15:30 to 16:47, so although playing times for the piece seem fairly consistent, you'll have to adjust for the one you're listening to.

Sections and Timings in the Great Fugue, Op. 133

1. Overtura: thematic "table of contents"
2. First fugue, 0:54: leaping, athletic fugue subject
3. Second fugue, 4:50: softer, murmuring textures
4. March and third fugue, 7:36: bouncy march, fugue subject in cello at about 8:08; reprise of second fugue theme at 11:23
5. March and coda, 12:34: same bouncy march; thematic recap at about 14:24, followed by climactic coda

The Overtura sets the fierce tone for the whole work. It's a sequence of abrupt, discrete musical gestures. But though the first-time listener can't know this, it's actually a table of contents of the thematic material, of which there is in fact remarkably little, from which the Great Fugue is built. The composer gets things going with a mighty leap for the full ensemble, which then roars out the four-note underlying theme, close kin to the opening ideas of Op. 132 and Op. 131. There's a snarling trill—trills will dominate the third fugue—then come long, dramatic pauses interrupting the theme, which is presented in rising phrases in a forceful short-long rhythm also we'll hear much of later. The main idea returns in a new key and more tentative tone, as the sixteenth notes that will accompany the second fugue enter as well. As he does in the quartet's second finale, Beethoven starts in what turns out to be the wrong key; he finds the right one—B-flat major—with a whispered version of the underlying theme, broken by deliberate pauses.

Out of nowhere, the first violin presents the first fugue subject, a new, leaping idea in detached short-long notes that's harsh but also bracing once you get used to it, while the viola plays the second subject, which we just heard played softly a moment ago. That makes this a double fugue—one that's based on two subjects. Throughout this savage passage, Beethoven holds to a brutally high volume. And there's no question of comfort here—you'll have to adjust to its headlong pace, the bumps in its rhythm, and Beethoven's fearless dissonances. Midway through, hammered triplets take over, but the sound remains austere and grand; the composer then combines the triplets with the original, detached-note pattern. He also finds a new way to present the leaping subject in a short-short-long rhythmic presentation, which he develops for a while before bringing the triplets back. The first fugue has an open ending, which connects smoothly to the second fugue.

A slower tempo and a new key (G-flat major, for those keeping track) presents the new, smoother, second fugue, in which the second violin presents a flowing new idea as the viola repeats the primal four-note theme. Soothing sixteenth notes pulse along almost continuously in this passage, where Beethoven develops his ideas contrapuntally without embarking on a real fugue. But the lyrical treatment here offers relief to players and listeners still reeling from the asperities of the Overtura and the first fugue. Finally the ensemble plays the flowing idea in a loud and fervent incarnation before Beethoven reduces the sixteenth notes to a muttering unison for the full ensemble, low down in the instruments' ranges.

A springy march in 6/8 rather than the 4/4 meter common to the genre begins; it's in the same rhythm as the rising short-long phrases from the Overtura. (This is the fourth section if you're subdividing the piece into ten parts.) Its tone seems brisk and cheery enough, compared with some of what we've heard, but it's tight and tough in its own way. This is interrupted by the third fugue, in A-flat major, the fifth of the subdivided sections. A tremendously potent passage that lies at the heart of the Great Fugue, it is also the toughest to crack, as you'll hear in the subject, stated by the cello, and the three-note short-long-short countersubject. A trill enters, again initiated by the cello, the snarling sound of which gradually comes to dominate the texture. The slashing eighth notes that enter in the violins introduce a wild, new force, and finally the thicket of trills tightens its grip on the passage.

The sound of the second violin shooting upward as though trying to break out signals a new section (the sixth subdivision) and a slight change of tone. The rising figure is in fact a compression of the work's primal four-note idea. You'll note the entrance of the leaping subject of the first fugue, which now does battle with the compressed motto-theme and eventually the subject and countersubject of the A-flat major fugue. Beethoven leads this to an unexpected and climactic review of the theme and accompaniment of the second fugue—subdivision seven—in which every note of that rich theme is hammered out with great force and feeling. It settles down on a series of equally unexpected shuddering trills for the cello under harmonically uncertain chords for the other three instruments. An extended return of the 6/8 march (subdivision eight) ensues that quietly contains the beginning of the coda (subdivisions nine and ten). A clearing of the harmonic and rhythmic atmospheres leads to a pause, after which several thematic ideas are presented and passed over, though not rejected in the manner of the last movement of the Ninth Symphony. What was a table of contents in the Overtura returns as a thematic index, over which the motto-theme triumphs, roared out decisively by the full ensemble. Some temporizing trills take over; then, atop a throbbing accompaniment for the viola, the violin sings out the leaping subject of the first fugue in an impassioned transfiguration as the second violin and cello play the motto-theme below; Beethoven ends the work ends swiftly on a cadence that is one of his most powerful.

The Late Quartets
C-sharp Minor, Op. 131,
and F Major, Op. 135

The two last quartets, in C-sharp Minor, Op. 131, and F Major, Op. 135, were completed in 1826, the last full year of Beethoven's life, with the C-sharp Minor begun late in 1825. They are two of his greatest quartets, although they differ radically in character. The C-sharp Minor may be the most daring of all Beethoven's works; at the least, it shares that title with the Great Fugue. The F Major Quartet represents Beethoven's final look back at classicism and a scaling back in length and scope, but its beauties and depths are not to be overlooked.

Beethoven dedicated the C-sharp Minor Quartet to Baron Joseph von Stutterheim, who had earned Beethoven's deep gratitude when he accepted the composer's troubled nephew, Karl, into his army regiment. For Beethoven personally, 1826 was one of the worst years in his life, culminating in Karl's attempted suicide in August—an event that was devastating to the composer. The detachment from events demanded by the composition of this great work is again worth noting: it's one of the last but most remarkable examples of Beethoven's ability to isolate his work from his personal life. Despite having completed the Galitzin commission of three quartets, he had more—a great deal more—to say in the genre. Beethoven died before the work could be performed, and its novelty and technical difficulties initially posed a barrier to players. The gravely ill Schubert asked to hear Op. 131, which was played for him five days before his death in November 1828. Recalled Karl Holz, "He fell into such a state of excitement and enthusiasm that we were all frightened for him."[1]

Beethoven considered Op. 131 his best quartet and, after joking to his publisher that it was "stolen from bits of this and that," said that the work showed "less lack of fantasy [imagination] than ever before." Ever since the late quartets became part of the standard repertory for that ensemble, Beethoven's appraisal has never been disputed, and Op. 131 has trailed superlatives in its wake. The C-sharp Minor has not only been called Beethoven's best string quartet, but the greatest of all works in the genre, and has even been called the masterwork of all the composer's many masterworks.

As you'll hear, much of Op. 131 is quick and light—Beethoven's wild humor is often evident, especially in the fourth and fifth movements—and at the same time, a deep lyricism marks every page of the quartet. But the overall character of the work must be taken as tragic in the highest sense, in that it reflects Beethoven's tragic vision. The outer movements (the first and seventh) define that character. Whatever the slow opening fugue expresses cannot be construed as joyous; and the sixth and seventh movements fulfill its prophecy in music of sorrow and struggle. The finale, the movement toward which the first six build, is perhaps Beethoven's grandest, and at times most terrifying, leaving little doubt as to the nature of the work as a whole. The music also seems to trace a process of incarnation, from purest spirit to more earthly joys and sorrows: its textures gradually take on more weight, from the disembodied calm of the opening fugue to the dense and dark finale.

All this may come across as a bit intimidating, but you'll also hear as you listen that the work is beautiful in readily perceptible ways, and, as noted, that much of it moves quickly and is airy in texture. One of the most helpful ways to approach Op. 131 is with a grasp of its unusual structure, surely Beethoven's boldest. The seven movements are linked and played without pause. Each is different in form: the opening movement is a slow fugue; the second, a swift dance. The very short third movement is an operatically styled recitative, and the fourth, a theme with six variations, acts as its central pillar. The fifth movement is a three-part scherzo, and the sixth is a "shadow" slow movement. The finale is in sonata form. Two of the seven movements—the third and sixth—are quite short, serving as introductions to the movements that follow. Perhaps discussions of key structures make your eyes glaze over, but it's important to understand that the opening fugue and the finale, the pillars of the work, are in C-sharp minor, and that the movements in between follow a harmonically bold path that also contributes significantly to the sense of the work as a single arc that moves inevitably from beginning to end, satisfying the ear, mind, and spirit.

Beethoven deliberately employed many musical structures in Op. 131, but you'll note as you listen that the work is one of high unity. This is because some of the themes are reconfigurations of the same four notes. Beethoven also redeploys variants and fragments of the twelve-note subject of the opening fugue in the finale. All the late quartets are deep in thought and feeling, but the unity of Op. 131, which stems from Beethoven's marvelous solution to the formal challenge he set himself, seems to set it just a bit ahead of the others.

Written in an austere mood and remote in expression from everyday experience, the opening fugue will probably be the most difficult movement of the quartet for the first-timer to take in. There's really no way to get to know it except by approaching it with patience; you won't get it on the first hearing, or perhaps even the tenth, but eventually it will begin to make sense in its own time and on its own terms. Moving at a slow and steady pace for its entire eight minutes of playing time, the fugue is based on a winding twelve-note subject made up of two phrases: a desolate opening sequence of four notes, with a stabbing accent on the fourth, followed by eight that move at an even pace and express a calmer affect. This is the theme that casts its shadow over the whole quartet, and as you'll hear, Beethoven brings it back to great effect in the finale. The first violin makes the first statement, followed by the second violin, the viola, and the cello in stately procession. The slow pace of the music allows you to take in its unceasing beauty. Beethoven puts the subject through a variety of contrapuntal treatments, but what's most important to the serious new listener is the steady, calm manner in which Beethoven treats the theme, tightening a strand here, unraveling a bit there. You may want to listen for the passage about halfway through where the violins and then the lower strings treat the theme in the close imitations known as canons; or for the moment where the cello plays the theme in longer notes, which is called augmentation. But even if you studied counterpoint, you'd be no closer to describing the affect of this movement, which stands alone in Beethoven's oeuvre for its otherworldliness. Finally, the music drives powerfully, though at the same slow pace, toward the major key—you'll hear the cello unmistakably finding the bottom note of a richly droning C-sharp major chord as the fugue moves with quiet majesty toward its closing; but listen at the very end to the cello, followed by the viola and the first violin, when they rise up gently from their places as the way is prepared for the second movement, which follows without pause.

That movement, a lilting dance in a convincing tone of innocence, makes the composition sound as though born anew. It differs from the fugue in all conceivable ways, but chiefly in how its quick tempo and buoyant 6/8 meter blend in a softly rustling sound that contrasts with the slow and steady flow of the fugue. Yet the linkage of the two sections, fugue and dance, seems paradoxically, inexplicably tight. Textures here are transparent, although Beethoven thickens them just a bit toward the end. The great jump the master makes is in the movement's key of D major, which according to the conventions of the time should not have been chosen to follow the C-sharp minor and C-sharp major (at the very end) of the preceding movement; it is the same Neapolitan relationship we heard so much of in the Op. 95 quartet. In that work, Beethoven used this semitonal key relationship more conventionally—from passage to passage, to achieve dramatic or mysterious effects within a movement. To shift keys from one movement to the next in that way was all but unheard of, except for one case by the ever daring Haydn.[2] This powerful motion from C-sharp to D launches the remaining movements of the quartet on a cyclical harmonic journey through a key sequence that leads gravitationally back to the C-sharp minor of the finale. Nevertheless, you don't have to know much about harmony to hear the effectiveness of Beethoven's harmonic structure for the work, or to feel its power.

The third movement, the shortest in the quartet, is an amusing fragment that serves to introduce the big movement that follows. Like the fourth movement of Op. 132, it has two portions, a recitative-like opening in a sharp rhythm and mock-stern tone followed by a cadenza for the first violin and a mellowing affect as Beethoven modulates to the key (A major) of the wonderful theme-and-variations fourth movement. Although texturally complex, the mood of this centerpiece of the work remains benign, even joyful, throughout. There's no minor-key variation and hardly a passing cloud, as there are in the third movement of Op. 127, where Beethoven dives deeper than here. With the burden of profundity carried by the fugue and the finale, the composer keeps the inner movements light—miraculously so.

The tempo is moderate rather than slow, and the theme is beautiful and highly memorable: don't be surprised if one listening makes it a permanent part of your musical mental landscape. And the theme isn't just beautiful; it's charming, too, underpinned by a pizzicato cello line that pads along enchantingly below. The first variation compresses the melody, embellishing it with graceful runs for the first violin and cello, while its second half emphasizes a rocking rhythm. The second is an exquisitely humorous take on a country dance, where the middle strings chug along as Beethoven condenses the theme into a jazzy eight-note essence, traded between the violin and cello; the phrases are extended into long lines in the second half. Beethoven subjects another condensed and coy version of the melody to canonic treatment in the third variation, where the mood remains blissful even as the theme is handled more strictly. The second half of the variation is marked by chains of witty trills, all in canon, starting in the cello and moving sequentially up to the higher instruments. The fourth variation, in a slower tempo, is marked by long lines of great beauty, interrupted impishly by plucked notes and chords. Eventually the composer allows the long lines to dominate the texture, though he brings the pizzicati back at the end. The next variation is the most obscure and strange, with the theme squeezed down to its harmonic essence, sounding like a musette—a kind of bagpipe. Fragments of the melody rise periodically from the droning. Finally, the sixth variation opens the theme into phrases of immense length, underpinned by a charming wiggle for the cello. Though that wiggle keeps things from getting too serious, the sound is pure glory, and you may find yourself tuning in to its nearly ecstatic nature.

Now Beethoven has the ensemble trade graceful, nonthematic triplet runs and trills while shifting the harmony; finally he gets to the key most remote—F major—from his overarching structure, where the theme is rapped out plainly and excitedly; he then changes the harmony twice more, the second time back to A major. The first half of the theme is rendered by the second violin and viola with the utmost grace over a florid trilling for the first violin and a rowing figure for the cello. Suddenly Beethoven jumps back to F major, and finally to A once again for the playful final thematic fragment.

The interval that separates the fourth movement from the fifth— the scherzo—comes closest to a real break between movements in the grand arc of Op. 131, but it's only a brief, measured rest, not a closing cadence. The players keep their bows poised and play on. The great scherzo that follows is included as track 9 on the accompanying CD, followed by the sixth movement (CD Track 10) and the finale (CD Track 11), to give you a sense of the dimension and sweep of this extraordinary work.

A sputtering figure for the cello kicks off this joyous, high-velocity scherzo, perhaps the best example of Beethoven's ability to treat simple ideas complexly. The affect is unmistakably that of a grand jest. At 0:02 the full ensemble enters with the main theme, the second phrase of which comes at 0:11. The tunes and phrasing are naive and sometimes foursquare, but the driving pace and richly varied tempos, rhythmic presentations, dynamics, and instrumentation provide an endless stream of surprises. There are a couple of slowdowns in which the machine seems to run down, with the pace picking up again at 0:23; and the opening section is repeated from 0:41. At 1:11, a smooth new idea resembling a nursery tune is introduced by the violins; it is passed to the viola and cello at 1:24, and a new version that acts as a reply is stated by the full ensemble at 1:34. An even sillier theme, something like a child's taunt, enters in the first violin at 1:50 and is then distributed among the other instruments, concluding in a series of isolated pizzicati spread around the ensemble. The main theme returns (2:05), then the smooth nursery tune (2:43), then a new idea that takes off on the rhythm of the nursery tune, into which soaring passage Beethoven reintroduces the taunt. Another reprise of the main theme (4:02) is heard at a delicate pianissimo, followed by a masterful sequence beginning at 4:43, in which the nursery themes stumble over each other and the music

stops to get its bearings a few times. And the final, shortened appearance of the main tune at 4:57 is one of Beethoven's most daring ideas:
he instructs the players to bow on the bridges of their instruments,
creating an eerie scratching sonority that looks far ahead to Debussy
and later composers, for whom tone color would be a critical stylistic
element. The final cadence, a simple three-note play on E major, ends
the movement; three G-sharps, spanning two octaves, set the stage for
the sixth movement.

This, the last and finest of the master's "shadow" slow movements,
serves two purposes: it fills, briefly but satisfyingly, the need for a
heartfelt slow movement, which this quartet lacks, and it sets the stage
harmonically for the finale and the return to C-sharp minor (and major).
Theoretically, its two minutes' playing time would seem inadequate
to carry so heavy a burden; but it succeeds. It consists of a simple
repetition of the two melodic phrases, the first heard at the start and
the second at 0:18. The second phrase, with its characteristic dotted
rhythm and sighing affect, comes to dominate the structure. This short
passage is another reason Op. 131 must ultimately be heard as tragic,
although hardly a cloud crosses the horizon from the second movement
to the end of the fifth. Even after the long and jubilant scherzo, this
introduction reverses the polarity of movements two through five. It's
useful to know specifically that the G-sharp minor in which it's written
is the dominant key of the tonic, C-sharp minor, the harmonic home
base of the quartet. But it's crucial to understand more broadly that
the dominant key always creates a need for resolution in the tonic key
in the harmonic vocabulary of the classical era, and never with more
gravitational force than right here. At 1:45 the first violin's line coils
up, then down, in a grand, almost sculptural gesture, clearing the way
for the finale. Hearing the last three movements of Op. 131 on the CD
will give you some sense of the breadth of Beethoven's plan, but it's
essential to listen to the whole work from the beginning, in context,
in order to get the full, terrifying effect of the return to the home key,
even though last heard more than thirty minutes earlier.

The full quartet roars out a single C-sharp, followed by a dramatic
pause, then the fearsome, asymmetrical, six-note thunderclap, one of
the master's very potent thematic ideas, that opens this sonata-form

movement. Another fierce pause leads to its repetition and the rising and falling marchlike element, also of great power. At 0:20 the fugue theme is brought back in an unambiguously pathos-laden mode, quite different from its inscrutable face earlier. The glorious second theme, a falling scalar idea over rich E major harmony, enters at 0:53, as does another simple but majestic long-note theme (1:38) that assumes a greater burden as the movement goes on. The development, short but gripping, begins at 2:00; note the contained fury of the falling scales, which the composer marks *non ligato*—not tied, or in detached notes that sound as though spat out—starting at 2:10. Things fall apart at 2:30 in a fog of uncertain harmony and rhythm. But at 2:40 the recapitulation brings back the original argument in full force, including the long-note theme at 2:50. Beethoven maneuvers to D major, the Neapolitan interval, for the recurrence of the second theme, reprising the harmonic drama of the first two movements (3:35). But at 4:34, Beethoven tightens the noose once more in his return to C-sharp minor and the first theme.

The thematic war goes on in a mix of ecstasy and terror until 5:31, when the long-note theme reappears in its last, most extended, and grandest avatar, and shuddering scales, rising this time but again *non ligato*, seem to herald a climax. But, moving subtly in an unexpected direction, Beethoven dodges a climax, or even a cadence (6:05),[3] making things more ambiguous in every way, until the end. The driving energy of the movement vanishes as the remade fugue theme, now stated in an exhausted, falling version, returns over the fragmented main theme, which also sounds drained (6:08). The harmony moves quietly to C-sharp major (6:20) as dreamlike fragments of the main theme and march drift about. At 6:41, the tempo even slows perceptibly. Then, at 6:53, the original tempo returns, and the march comes back in sharply rising notes, leading to the three crunching C-sharp major chords that complete the cycle.

Prepare for this great ending to make you shiver. But ask yourself as well what this rise, fall, and brief rise again at the very end has in common with, for example, the endings of your favorite symphonies of the middle period, or, closer to home, the second and third "Razumovsky" Quartets. The answer is, not much. Those thunderous affirmations have given way to something far subtler, more ambivalent, and more ambiguous. Beethoven's daring conception and perfection of form in Op. 131 is well matched by the tragicomic scope of his ideas.

On the surface, the final quartet, in F major, Op. 135, could hardly differ more from its far-ranging predecessor. In it, Beethoven reverts to a four-movement format and a smaller scale, with a playing time of about twenty-three minutes, compared to the forty or so of Op. 131. Its style shows the composer in his brilliant post-classical manner, as in the Eighth Symphony, and its mood is predominantly relaxed and good-humored. But don't think for a moment that Op. 135 is a letdown or throwaway: it's an exquisite composition in which Beethoven pays urbane tribute to Haydn and Mozart. Although its formal ambitions may be more modest, its finish and workmanship seem to achieve a new level of sophistication, perhaps even surpassing its more earnest companion works among the late quartets. No less than the prior four, Op. 135 repays careful listening and long acquaintance.

Its moods are relaxed, playful, and humorous in the first movement and finale; wild and stormy in the second-movement scherzo (CD Track 12); and songful and utterly tranquil in the slow third movement. The first movement, in a textbook sonata form, consists of short but tightly packed thematic elements that have a comical tendency to fall down, and that the composer presents individually and without transitional material, moving from one to the other after, or sometimes without, a pause. The initial sequence, with its off-balance phrases, sets the playful mood. The opening theme, set over a charming walking bass line for the cello, turns out to be suspiciously short, and the smooth falling idea that follows is also witty but offers little hint as to what's around the corner. The second theme, rendered by the violins in dialogue, is more articulate and ends in triplets, which the composer makes an integral part of texture throughout the movement. The brief development opens with the falling idea, then drifts amusingly though faraway keys. Listen also for the comical grunts from the cello, echoed by other instruments, which may remind you of some of the decorative effects in the third movement of Op. 130 (CD Track 8). Perhaps the movement's greatest paradox is its casual and relaxed air, which adorns some of Beethoven's tightest thematic management and exquisite craftsmanship.

The wild second-movement scherzo is another story. Beethoven shows the unabated force of his imagination even in this last quartet, written just months before the onset of his final illness. Though in a standard three-part form, the music surges with excitement from the start, where the hopping main theme can be heard in the cello. At 0:09 the cello and viola insert a jarring low note while continuing the jumpy rhythm that marks every moment of the outer sections. At 0:14 the violin takes the theme; at 0:35 the section is repeated, going back to the jolting notes for the low instruments. The trio, which contains the most bizarre but stunning ideas in this movement, takes off at 1:00 with a turn for the violin; at 1:03 the fiddle's rising line suddenly takes a big jump, many more of which will follow. At 1:15 Beethoven changes key abruptly from F major to G major, a fine example of the Neapolitan interval. At 1:26 the turn initially stated by the violin asserts itself more firmly, and at 1:37, in one of Beethoven's most extraordinary passages, the violin soars above the turn, repeated forty-nine times without alteration, in a mad leaping dance, showing, if nothing else, the difference between the composer's consciousness and our own. At 2:02 the scherzo returns; a brief coda at 3:05 ends the movement.

The theme of the third movement, one of Beethoven's most tranquil lyrical statements, was originally intended for a role in Op. 131 but in the end wound up here. It's a melody of great, calm breadth with a vocal feeling whose rises and falls move with the natural flow of breathing. Beethoven treats it to four variations, the first staying close to the theme but ranging higher. The second, in C-sharp minor, the sibling tonality of the movement's D-flat major, moves gently, seeming to express a remembered pain. The third variation brings back the theme unaltered, adding some contrapuntal inflections that leave the lyric tone undisturbed; and in the fourth variation Beethoven finally subjects the tune to decoration in tender, broken phrases. If this quartet were better known, this poised, almost understated lento might gain the appreciation it deserves as the master's last utterance of its kind.

The finale, the most complex structure in Op. 135, is set to a motto theme in the score. The words *Muss es sein? Es muss sein! Es muss sein!* (Must it be? It must be! It must be!) are set to two of the movement's main thematic ideas. The portentous query and reply stem from a dialogue between the composer and a subscriber to his work, which Beethoven then turned into an inane joke with his publisher.[4] Like the first movement, his wonderful finale is lighthearted, with two mock doom-laden passages that play on the fatalistic-sounding motto-theme. The movement opens with an introduction in which the first, gloomy phrase is presented and paired first with flowing passagework, then with a sturdier three-note phrase. The brisk and cheerful version of the reply (*Es muss sein! Es muss sein!*) emerges, followed by a melting six-note tail. The second theme, worthy of Mozart, is an airy and insubstantial march tune such as one might hear in *The Magic Flute*, making one wonder how a bare handful of notes can be so beautiful and carry so much meaning. The development makes a feint at counterpoint, but the mood remains light and the expression filled with charm and humor. Later, though, the going gets a bit heavier; and when the full quartet shares a long trill, we know something is up. Beethoven brings back the introductory material, now louder and more menacing. But the mechanical sawing of the violins' tremolandi over the opening motto and allied phrases is unmistakably comical overstatement, and soon the brisk main theme comes back in its full, unaffected joy. The composer reprises the second theme in an even more enchanting pizzicato version decorated by high, mincing quarter notes for the first violin, then ends the quartet on a magnificent but trim cadence based on the *Es muss sein!* phrase.

Listening to Beethoven's Chamber Music

The new listener to Beethoven's chamber works faces a challenge nearly as daunting as getting to know the Great Fugue, of which eighty-eight performances are offered on the Arkivmusic.com Web site. Finding recordings that clarify, satisfy, and inspire is a marvelous lifetime job for a dedicated listener. Beethoven's works for chamber ensemble must be the most widely recorded of any composer's.

For my money, the best complete set of the violin sonatas overall is the well-known and venerated one with Arthur Grumiaux and the pianist Clara Haskil. One of the best violinists of the twentieth century, Grumiaux had a glorious tone and an aristocratic reserve that served everything he played well; unlike many fiddlers, there was never a hint of schmaltz about his playing. And the revered Haskil was an uncompetitive but sublime interpretive partner. Their recordings of Mozart violin sonatas are also hard to beat. A more recent set I've also enjoyed is that with the violinist Augustin Dumay and the pianist Maria-João Pires. They tend to employ very quick tempos, which these high-energy scores take to readily. Fine older recordings of individual sonatas include three (Op. 24, Op. 30 No. 3, and Op. 47) with the violinist Henryk Szeryng and Arthur Rubinstein. A performance of the "Kreutzer" Sonata from a 1940 recital at the Library of Congress with Joseph Szigeti and Béla Bartók on piano is not to be missed. In the case of the cello sonatas I own only one recording—that of the cellist Pierre Fournier and the great Beethoven pianist Artur Schnabel. Other performances, particularly those by the Russian giants Mstislav Rostropovich on cello and Sviatoslav Richter on piano, are brilliant too, and you will certainly not go wrong with that duo.

I came to the piano trios through the fine set from the 1960s and '70s of the Stern-Rose-Istomin Trio, which has held up well. I don't know those of the Beaux Arts Trio, but if their recordings of the Haydn and Mozart piano trios are any indication, their Beethoven trios should be a safe bet. There's also a recording of the "Archduke" Trio by the Heifetz-Feuermann-Rubinstein ensemble that I've enjoyed. The deluxe ensemble for the string trios on the market, featuring the violinist Anne-Sophie Mutter, the violist Bruno Giuranna, and Rostropovich on cello, is all one could expect. However, those by the members of the Kodály Quartet (the second violinist takes the day off) on Naxos, whose performances of the quartets are sampled on the CD here, sound every bit as good to me in this relatively unfamiliar repertory.

There are two performances of the Piano and Wind Quintet, Op. 16, in my collection. The first, with members of the English Chamber Orchestra and the pianist Murray Perahia, is the first I came to know, and still sounds good. But another I've loved recently features the all-time great horn player Dennis Brain in the wind group and the composer Benjamin Britten on piano. The playing is gorgeous and the music making as sensitive as it can be.

Of course, the string quartets are the big game here. I grew up on those by the Budapest Quartet from the 1960s, which sound impressive on vinyl but seem no longer to be in release—a terrible omission that whichever musical conglomerate has the rights to them now should rectify. I have also liked the Tokyo String Quartet's recordings, particularly of the early quartets, which are always a challenge to make interesting; and their Op. 18 set includes a fine performance of the underappreciated String Quintet, Op. 29, with Pinchas Zukerman on second viola. The middle and late quartets in the recordings by the Alban Berg Quartet are also fine, and I have enjoyed several recordings by the Quartetto Italiano. The performances by the Yale Quartet are also very good. Before writing this book I had not heard those of the Kodály Quartet on Naxos, featured on the compact disc, but they are absolutely excellent, to me as good as any. I've recently become acquainted with the Hagen Quartet's astonishing performance of the "Serioso," and so I'm planning to explore their series further.

Some time around 1990 I bought the Talich Quartet's recordings of the middle and late quartets, and ever since I have loved this Czech ensemble's enormous energy and rhythmic drive; but those who need fat string sound should know in advance that their tone is not overly rich. The players' energy always comes through, though. Finally, I've recently enjoyed the late quartets played by the Hollywood Quartet, an ensemble consisting of four remarkable soloists who worked in Los Angeles in the 1950s and '60s. Don't let the improbable name mislead you: these are not just four great individual players but a magnificent, instinctive ensemble. They recorded a number of other chamber works, as well, and anything the Hollywood did is worth hearing.

Notes

Chapter 1

1. Keller, *The Great Haydn Quartets*.

Chapter 2

1. Quoted in Lockwood, *Beethoven: The Music and the Life*, p. 47.
2. Quoted in ibid., p. 50.
3. Cooper, *Beethoven*, pp. 52–53.
4. Lockwood, *Beethoven*, p. 196.
5. Ibid., pp. 300–301.
6. Ibid., p. 233.
7. Cf. Cooper, *Beethoven*, p. 376.
8. von Breuning, p. 44.
9. Quoted in Lockwood, *Beethoven*, p. 197.
10. Cooper, *Beethoven*, pp. 153–54, 247, and 333.
11. von Breuning, p. 72.

Chapter 3

1. Rosen, *The Classical Style*, pp. 329–50.

Chapter 4

1. Solomon, *Beethoven*, p. 250.
2. Watson, p. 206.

Chapter 6

1. Rosen, *The Classical Style*, pp. 351–65.
2. Cooper, *Beethoven*, p. 61.
3. Lockwood, *Beethoven*, p. 304.
4. *Oxford Dictionary of Music*, p. 831
5. Cooper, *Beethoven*, p. 216.
6. Hurwitz, p. 28.
7. Watson, p. 56.
8. Joseph Kerman, *The Beethoven Quartets*, p. 71.

Chapter 7

1. Watson, p. 76.
2. Cooper, p. 72.
3. Quoted by Lockwood, p. 109.

Chapter 8

1. Lockwood and the Juilliard String Quartet, *Inside Beethoven's Quartets*, p. 10.

Chapter 9

1. Kerman, *The Beethoven Quartets*, p. 85.
2. Quoted in *The Beethoven Quartet Companion*, p. 151.
3. Cooper, p. 99. Readers interested in hearing the "Amenda" version of Op. 18 No. 1 will have to look hard for a recording. The only performance of the complete four-movement quartet I'm aware of is by the Mendelssohn Quartet, but I have not heard it. The first movement of both versions, played by the Juilliard Quartet, are on the compact disc that accompanies the very fine study *Inside Beethoven's Quartets*, by Lewis Lockwood and the Juilliard Quartet, listed in the bibliography. The differences are astonishing, with the "Amenda" version of the movement running more than four minutes longer than the revised one.
4. Kinderman, "Transformational Processes in Beethoven's Op. 18 Quartets," p. 13.

5. Michael Steinberg, "The Early Quartets," in *The Beethoven Quartet Companion*, p. 151.
6. Lockwood, *Beethoven*, p. 165.
7. Kerman, p. 52
8. Quoted by Kerman, pp. 65–71.
9. Cooper, p. 101; Lockwood, *Beethoven*, p. 165.
10. Cooper, p. 100.
11. Kerman, p. 76.
12. Steinberg, *The Beethoven Quartet Companion*, p. 145.
13. Steinberg, p. 147.

Chapter 10

1. Kerman, pp. 100–101.
2. Solomon, *Beethoven*, p. 260.
3. Kerman, p. 106.
4. Watson, p. 150.
5. Lockwood and the Juilliard String Quartet, *Inside Beethoven's Quartets*, pp. 97–98.
6. Steinberg, *The Beethoven Quartet Companion*, p. 189.

Chapter 11

1. Watson, pp. 177–79.
2. Marston, "'Haydn's Geist aus Beethoven's Händen'? Fantasy and Farewell in Quartet in E-flat, Op. 74," in *The String Quartets of Beethoven*, pp. 109–31.
3. Ibid.
4. Quoted in Lockwood, *Beethoven*, p. 325.

Chapter 12

1. Watson, pp. 226–27.
2. Steinberg, *The Beethoven Quartet Companion*, pp. 218–19.
3. Kerman, p. 224.
4. Cooper, p. 354.
5. Kerman, pp. 242–50.

Chapter 13

1. Cooper, *Beethoven*, p. 355.
2. Cooper, p. 358.
3. Solomon, *Beethoven*, p. 422.
4. Kerman, pp. 370–71.
5. Kerman, p. 313–14.
6. See Lockwood, *Beethoven*, pp. 463–65.

Chapter 14

1. Solomon, *Beethoven*, p. 417.
2. See Lockwood, *Beethoven*, p. 470; it's Haydn's final piano sonata, the E-flat Major of 1794, the second movement of which is in E major.
3. Kinderman, "Beethoven's Last Quartets," in *The String Quartets of Beethoven*, pp. 311–15.
4. Kerman, p. 362.

Selected Bibliography

Beethoven, Ludwig van. *Complete String Quartets from the Breitkopf & Härtel Edition*. New York: Dover, 1970.

————. *Six Great Piano Trios from the Breitkopf & Härtel Edition*. New York: Dover, 1987.

————. *Complete Violin Sonatas from the Breitkopf & Härtel Edition*. New York: Dover, 1990.

————. *Sonaten für Klavier und Violoncello*. Score edited by Jens Dufner. Munich: G. Henle, 2009.

————. *Klaviertrios, Band II*. Study score. Edited by Günter Raphael. Munich: G. Henle, 1983.

————. *Quintet in E-flat Major, Op. 16 for Piano, Oboe, Clarinet, Horn, and Bassoon*. New York: International Music, n.d.

————. *Streichquintette*. Study score. Edited by Sabine Kurth. Munich: G. Henle, 2001.

————. *Streichtrios und Streichduo*. Study score. Edited by Emil Platen. Munich: G. Henle, 1993.

————. *Septett in Es-dur Opus 20*. Study score. Edited by Egon Voss. Munich: G. Henle, 2008.

Cooper, Barry. *Beethoven*. Oxford: Oxford University Press, 2008.

Hurwitz, David. *Getting the Most Out of Mozart: The Instrumental Works*. Pompton Plains, NJ: Amadeus Press, 2005.

Keller, Hans. *The Great Haydn Quartets: Their Interpretation*. London: J. M. Dent, 1986.

Kennedy, Michael, ed. *The Oxford Dictionary of Music*. Second ed. Oxford: Oxford University Press, 1994.

Kerman, Joseph. *The Beethoven Quartets*. New York: W.W. Norton, 1966.

Kinderman, William, ed. *The String Quartets of Beethoven*. Urbana: University of Illinois Press, 2006.

Libbey, Ted. *The NPR Listener's Encyclopedia of Classical Music*. New York: Workman, 2006.

Lockwood, Lewis. *Beethoven: The Music and the Life*. New York: W. W. Norton, 2003.

Lockwood, Lewis, and the Juilliard String Quartet. *Inside Beethoven's Quartets: History, Performance, Interpretation*. Cambridge, MA: Harvard University Press, 2008.

Lockwood, Lewis, and Mark Kroll, eds. *The Beethoven Violin Sonatas: History, Criticism, Performance*. Urbana: University of Illinois Press, 2004.

Mozart, Wolfgang Amadeus. *Quintett für Klavier und Blaser, KV 452*. Study score. Edited by Wolf-Dieter Seiffert. Munich: G. Henle, 2000.

Rosen, Charles. *The Classical Style: Haydn, Mozart, Beethoven*. New York: W. W. Norton, 1972.

Solomon, Maynard. *Beethoven*. New York: Schirmer Trade Books, 2001.

————. *Late Beethoven*. Berkeley and Los Angeles: University of California Press, 2003.

Tolstoy, Leo. *The Death of Ivan Ilyich and Other Stories*. Translated by Richard Pevear and Larissa Volokhonsky. New York: Alfred A. Knopf, 2009.

Tovey, Donald Francis. *Chamber Music*. Oxford: Oxford University Press, 1989.

von Breuning, Gerhard. *Memories of Beethoven*. Edited by Maynard Solomon. Translated by Henry Mins and Maynard Solomon. Cambridge: Cambridge University Press, 1992.

Watson, Angus. *Beethoven's Chamber Music in Context*. Woodbridge, UK: Boydell Press, 2010.

Winter, Robert, and Robert Martin, editors. *The Beethoven Quartet Companion*. Berkeley and Los Angeles: University of California Press, 1994.

CD Track Listing

1. Sonata for Piano and Violin in G Major, Op. 30 No. 3:
   Allegro assai (first movement) (6:26)
   Takako Nishizaki, violin; Jenö Jandó, piano
   From Naxos CD 8.550286

2. Sonata for Piano and Cello in G Minor, Op. 5 No. 2: Rondo:
   Allegro (second movement) (9:03)
   Csaba Onczay, cello; Jenö Jandó, piano
   From Naxos CD 8.550479

3. Trio for Piano, Violin and Cello in B-flat Major ("Archduke")
   Op. 97: Andante cantabile ma però con moto (third movement)
   (11:48)
   Stuttgart Piano Trio
   From Naxos CD 8.550949

4. String Quartet in B-flat Major, Op. 18 No. 6; Scherzo: Allegro
   (third movement) (3:28)
   Kodály Quartet
   From Naxos CD 8.550560

5. String Quartet in F Major ("Razumovsky"), Op. 59 No. 1:
   Allegro (first movement) (10:42)
   Kodály Quartet
   From Naxos CD 8.554181

6. String Quartet in F Minor ("Quartetto serioso"), Op. 95:
   Allegro con brio (first movement) (4:37)
   Kodály Quartet
   From Naxos CD 8.554181

7. String Quartet in B-flat Major, Op. 130: Presto
   (second movement) (2:04)

   Kodály Quartet
   From Naxos CD 8.554593

8. String Quartet in B-flat Major, Op. 130: Andante con moto ma
   non troppo (third movement) (6:28)

   Kodály Quartet
   From Naxos CD 8.554593

9. String Quartet in C-sharp Minor, Op. 131: Presto
   (fifth movement) (5:17)

   Kodály Quartet
   From Naxos CD 8.554594

10. String Quartet in C-sharp Minor, Op. 131: Adagio quasi un poco
    andante (sixth movement) (2:02)

    Kodály Quartet
    From Naxos CD 8.554594

11. String Quartet in C-sharp Minor, Op. 131: Allegro
    (seventh movement) (7:06)

    Kodály Quartet
    From Naxos CD 8.554594

12. String Quartet in F Major, Op. 135: Vivace (second movement)
    (3:16)

    Kodály Quartet
    From Naxos CD 8.554594